# Learn WPF M
# XAML, C# and the MVVM pattern

Be ready for coding away next week using WPF and MVVM

Arnaud Weil

# Learn WPF MVVM - XAML, C# and the MVVM pattern

Be ready for coding away next week using WPF and MVVM

Arnaud Weil

ISBN 978-1-326-84799-9

© 2016 - 2017 Arnaud Weil

*To my parents, for teaching me freedom and making sure I can enjoy it.*

*To my wonderful family. Your love and support fueled this book.*

*To my readers who suggested improvements to this book, especially Doğan Kartaltepe.*

# Contents

1. **Introduction** . . . . . . . . . . . . . . . . . . . . . . 1
   1.1 What this book is not . . . . . . . . . . . . 1
   1.2 Prerequisites . . . . . . . . . . . . . . . . . 1
   1.3 How to read this book . . . . . . . . . . . 2
   1.4 Tools you need . . . . . . . . . . . . . . . . 2
   1.5 Source code . . . . . . . . . . . . . . . . . . 3

2. **Why WPF ?** . . . . . . . . . . . . . . . . . . . . . . . 5

3. **Creating a WPF application** . . . . . . . . . . . . 15
   3.1 Developer - designer workflow . . . . . . 15
   3.2 Editors . . . . . . . . . . . . . . . . . . . . . 16
   3.3 Adding a control . . . . . . . . . . . . . . . 17
   3.4 Simple controls . . . . . . . . . . . . . . . . 18
   3.5 Navigation . . . . . . . . . . . . . . . . . . . 26
   3.6 It's your turn to code: do-it-yourself . . . 28
   3.7 Exercise - Create the application and contact page . . . . . . . . . . . . . . . . . . . . 30
   3.8 Exercise solution . . . . . . . . . . . . . . . 31
   3.9 Understanding XAML . . . . . . . . . . . . 33
   3.10 Events . . . . . . . . . . . . . . . . . . . . . . 42

# CONTENTS

    3.11 Exercise - Create the menu page . . . . . 44
    3.12 Exercise solution . . . . . . . . . . . . . . 44
    3.13 Layout . . . . . . . . . . . . . . . . . . . . 46
    3.14 List controls . . . . . . . . . . . . . . . . . 60
    3.15 Exercise - Create the discussion page . . 63
    3.16 Exercise solution . . . . . . . . . . . . . . 65

4. **Managing data in a WPF application** . . . . . . **69**
   - 4.1 Data binding . . . . . . . . . . . . . . . . . 69
   - 4.2 DataContext . . . . . . . . . . . . . . . . . 75
   - 4.3 Converters . . . . . . . . . . . . . . . . . . 77
   - 4.4 Displaying collections using list controls . 79
   - 4.5 Customizing list controls . . . . . . . . . . 81
   - 4.6 Exercise - Display messages from a data object . . . . . . . . . . . . . . . . . . . . 85
   - 4.7 Exercise solution . . . . . . . . . . . . . . 87
   - 4.8 INotifyPropertyChanged . . . . . . . . . . 90
   - 4.9 INotifyCollectionChanged . . . . . . . . . 93
   - 4.10 Exercise - Display products and details . 94
   - 4.11 Exercise solution . . . . . . . . . . . . . . 96

5. **Making it shine: customize the look** . . . . . . **101**
   - 5.1 Change a control's look . . . . . . . . . . 101
   - 5.2 Exercise - Create a basic button template 106
   - 5.3 Exercise solution . . . . . . . . . . . . . . 107
   - 5.4 Resources . . . . . . . . . . . . . . . . . . 108
   - 5.5 Exercise - Set the background . . . . . . 112
   - 5.6 Exercise solution . . . . . . . . . . . . . . 112
   - 5.7 Styles . . . . . . . . . . . . . . . . . . . . 114
   - 5.8 Exercise - Improve menu page using an implicit style . . . . . . . . . . . . . . . . . 118

|   |      |                                        |     |
|---|------|----------------------------------------|-----|
|   | 5.9  | Exercise solution . . . . . . . . . . . . | 118 |
|   | 5.10 | Themes . . . . . . . . . . . . . . . . . | 119 |
|   | 5.11 | Transforms . . . . . . . . . . . . . . . | 120 |
|   | 5.12 | Control states . . . . . . . . . . . . . | 122 |
|   | 5.13 | Animations . . . . . . . . . . . . . . . | 125 |
| **6.** | **MVVM pattern for WPF** . . . . . . . . . . | **129** |
|   | 6.1  | Spaghetti code . . . . . . . . . . . . . | 129 |
|   | 6.2  | MVC . . . . . . . . . . . . . . . . . . | 131 |
|   | 6.3  | MVVM . . . . . . . . . . . . . . . . . | 132 |
|   | 6.4  | Recommended steps (simple) . . . . . . | 133 |
|   | 6.5  | Example . . . . . . . . . . . . . . . . | 140 |
|   | 6.6  | Example, more complex . . . . . . . . . | 143 |
|   | 6.7  | Commands and methods . . . . . . . . | 148 |
|   | 6.8  | Recommended steps (complete) . . . . . | 152 |
|   | 6.9  | Exercise - Display products and details using MVVM . . . . . . . . . . . . . . . | 153 |
|   | 6.10 | Exercise solution . . . . . . . . . . . . | 154 |
|   | 6.11 | MVVM frameworks in short . . . . . . . | 160 |

**A word from the author** . . . . . . . . . . . . . . . . **163**

**The Learn collection** . . . . . . . . . . . . . . . . . . **165**

# 1. Introduction

## 1.1 What this book is not

I made my best to keep this book small, so that you can learn WPF quickly without getting lost in petty details. If you're looking for a reference book where you'll find answers to all the questions you may have within the next 4 years of your WPF practice, you'll find other heavy books for that.

My purpose is to swiftly provide you with the tools you need to code your first WPF application using the MVVM pattern and be able to look for more by yourself when needed. While some authors seems to pride themselves in having the thickest book, in this series I'm glad I achieved the thinnest possible book for my purpose. Though I tried my best to keep all of what seems necessary, based on my 14 years experience of teaching.

I assume that you know what WPF is and when to use it. In case you don't, read the following *Why WPF ?* chapter.

## 1.2 Prerequisites

In order for this book to meet its goals, you must :

# 2　　　　　　　　　　　　　　　　　　　　Introduction

- Have basic experience creating an application with C# (any type of application is alright).
- Have working knowledge of Visual Studio.
- Have basic knowledge of XML syntax.
- Have basic knowledge of SQL Server.

> You could as well use VB.NET to code a WPF application. I chose to include only C# code in that book because I want it small and my field experience shows that almost every teams chooses C# over VB.NET nowadays.

## 1.3 How to read this book

This book's aim is to make you productive as quickly as possible. For this we'll use some theory, several demonstrations, plus exercises. Exercises appear like the following:

> ✏️ Do it yourself: Time to grab your keyboard and code away to meet the given objectives.

## 1.4 Tools you need

The only tool you'll need to work through that book is Visual Studio 2015. You can get any of those editions:

- Visual Studio 2015 Community (free)
- Visual Studio 2015 Professional

## 1.5 Source code

All of the source code for the demos and do-it-yourself solutions is available at https://bitbucket.org/epobb/learnwpfexercises

It can be downloaded as a ZIP file[1], or if you installed GIT you can simply type:

```
git clone https://bitbucket.org/epobb/learnwpfexercis\
es.git
```

---

[1] https://bitbucket.org/epobb/learnwpfexercises/downloads

# 2. Why WPF ?

If you're in a hurry, you can safely skip this chapter and head straight to the Creating a WPF application chapter. This *Why WPF* chapter is there for those that want to know why WPF should be used.

WPF is a .NET development framework for desktop applications that solves several problems encountered with previous development frameworks.

## Applications were counter-intuitive

Do you remember Windows XP? In order to turn off the computer, you had to press a button titled *Start*. Not really intuitive, is it? While this is a mainstream example, most software suffered from bad user experience: it was simply too complicated for a user to find her way around.

Some programs were even so complicated to use that a *wizard* was run when launched in order to guide users through the process of using the application. Wait: "process"? Using an application shouldn't be a *process*. It shouldn't be complicated to use an application, in fact the application should adapt to the user. While that debate would be nice for UX experts, my point is: why were applications so complicated to use?

The answer to that question is rooted within that simple fact: developers were asked to design the user-experience using code. Why? Because in many technology stacks, the user experience is *coded* by a developer, not *drawn* by a UX expert. Now, how can we expect someone to work correctly using inappropriate tools and lacking the necessary knowledge? A developer has little knowledge of user experience, and a programming language is not an appropriate way to create a user interface.

It all comes down to this: user-experience shouldn't be created using code, and it should be designed by a UX expert.

## Applications were dull

Here is an application I used for accounting:

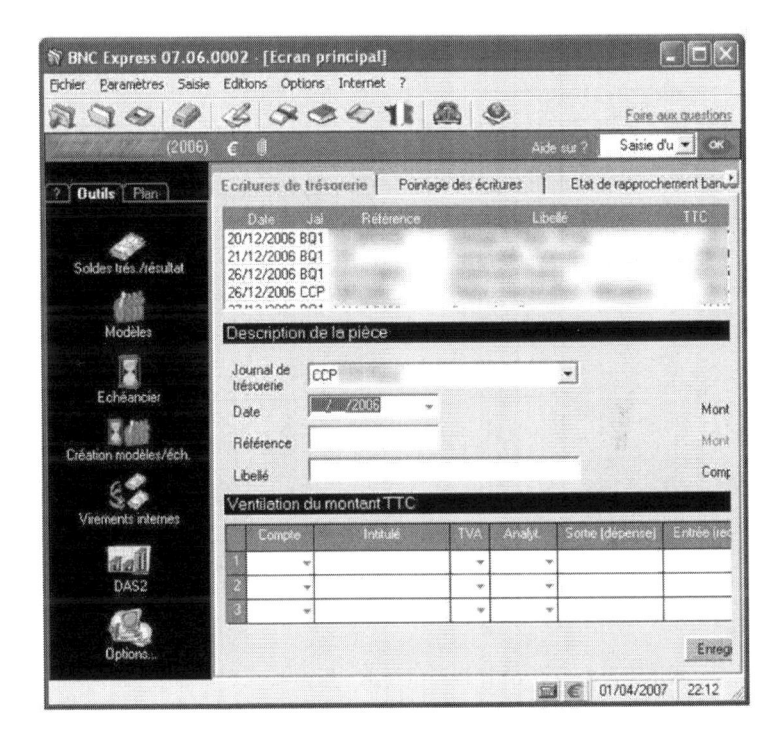

Alright, the program did the job it was supposed to do. But oh my, what a dull interface. Plus it's not appealing at all. It doesn't handle resizes correctly, doesn't fill the available screen estate, and it looks like the icons were randomly picked. No need to tell you that I wasn't eager to use that program as often as I needed to.

But it would be too easy to blame the developer for that application's dullness. Coding a nice UI could easily double development time when using frameworks like Windows Forms, because you have to *code* in order to handle:

- Resizing
- Homogeneity
- Styling
- Elements positioning

Another source for that dullness is the fact that few developers have design skills. And vice-versa.

## Nice GUIs could be dreamed of but not implemented

When you watch a movie or your favorite series, look at the user interface when people use computers. Did you notice how well designed, fluid and attractive they are? When some evil hacker tries to enter a system, he just has to press a big shiny "Hack" button. And when the hero shows the President some exceptional event live, she just slides through the information, zooms in and out in a fluid manner.

Same goes with Tom Cruise in Minority Report: in order to browse through files, he just moves around the pictures and movies using gestures:

What does it mean? That people who can create attractive, intuitive, user-friendly IHMs exist. However they work for movies, not for the computer industry. Why, you ask? Well, they were fed up with us developers.

Just think about the latest time some designer (or any creative people for that matter) came in and asked "hey, it would be great if there was a floating unicorn and when you pulled the hair it would float around and [add whatever you need here]". What did you answer? Probably something that goes along those lines: "it's not possible". But what you really meant was: "it's not possible to do so in a time that is reasonable, since it would take more time to code than the business logic itself". And you were right, because your framework didn't allow you to do so.

So do you know what happened? Those creative people got tired of seeing their ideas teared down and they went to work somewhere else. At some place where they wouldn't hear "no" as the only answer to their ideas. Movies, series, you name it.

## Appearance and logic separation

When Windows Forms, MFC C++, Java Swing or other client application frameworks were designed, the developers did what seemed natural to them: use the coding language in order to describe the user interface. For instance, a UI in Windows Forms is described using C# or VB.NET:

**Windows Forms example of a UI description**

```
public class Form1 : Form
{
  public Form1()
  {
    Button b = new Button();
    b.Text = "Buy stocks";
    b.Left = 20;
    b.Top = 40;
    b.Click += new EventHandler(b_Click);
  }
  void b_Click(object sender, EventArgs e)
  {
      // ...
  }
}
```

In the example above the button creation, position and appearance are set using C#. Which brings two problems:

1. A designer cannot edit this code. Even if she had

the knowledge to do so, would you allow a designer to edit C# code?
2. A quick look at that code doesn't give a clue about the button appearance. Which makes any design work harder.

In fact, we all know that **presentation code and logical code should not be mixed**. But Windows Forms made the mistake. And many other frameworks did.

## The WPF solution

In the HTML world, problems aren't so tough: designers work on the appearance while coders work on the business logic. Why is it so? Simply because things are separated: designers work in HTML and CSS files that describe the appearance, while developers work in JavaScript files. Plus HTML and CSS are quite adequate for describing an appearance.

Microsoft took the same approach with WPF. But HTML would have been too limited for desktop applications so they simply created XAML. XAML (XML application markup language) is XML, and you can think of it as HTML on steroids.

Since mixing presentation code and logical code was an error, WPF separates them. For each screen we have two files:

- a XAML file, describing the appearance, including any animation;

- a C# file, describing the functional logic of the screen. That file is called *code-behind*.

Practically, when you create a screen named *MyScreen*, it will be made of two files: MyScreen.xaml (appearance) and MyScreen.xaml.cs (code-behind).

Using separate files makes everything better: designers and developers can work on the same project, each on their own files.

Apart from this separation, WPF also introduced the following features:

- Controls composition: most controls can host other controls. For instance you can have buttons inside a ListBox control , or any shape and even video inside a Button control.
- Adaptation to any screen resolution: when working with pixels as in Windows Forms, programs get smaller as the resolution rises. WPF uses device-independent pixels, that state the real size independently of the screen resolution.

## What does it all mean?

WPF simply allows for gorgeous user interfaces, which can be created before, during, or after the business logic is written. This allows for instance for a prototype to be turned into an application just by adding the business logic in C#.

XAML being very flexible, most of the design work that would have taken weeks using previous frameworks is done in hours. For instance, adding close buttons to tabs in Windows Forms takes 5 days, but doing so in WPF is a matter of minutes even though the TabControl didn't include them.

## XAML

Though it can easily be used by a designer, XAML is an extremely powerful tool. Being XML-based, it can cope with several XAML-specific or XML tools:

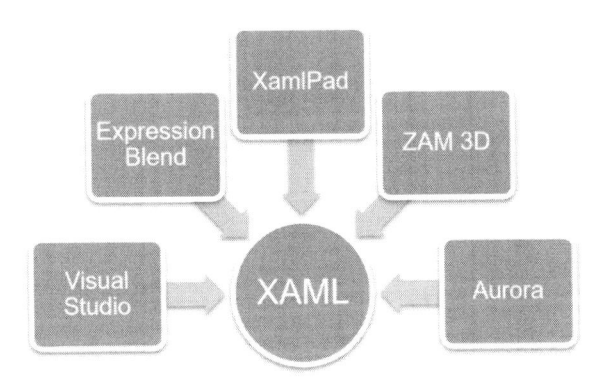

One feature that makes XAML so powerful is that it is a very easy way to instantiate .NET classes. More about that in the Understanding XAML chapter.

# 3. Creating a WPF application

## 3.1 Developer - designer workflow

When working on a WPF application there are two roles:

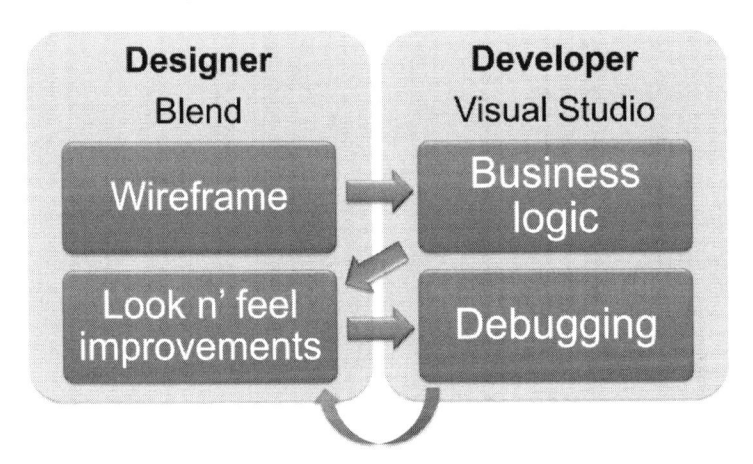

The designer is in charge of creating the wireframe and then high quality version of the user interface. The developer is in charge of coding the business logic, connecting with data and, well, um... debugging.

I'm talking about *roles* here. On a small team, the developers themselves could take the the *designer* role. On a large team however, it's a good idea to have separate people in charge of those roles. Simply because a developer is not a designer. Though this book is going to teach you how to use the designer tools, you'll realize that using a hammer doesn't make you a craftsman. Designing nice user interfaces has its own learning curve.

In fact, I've been very impressed by the designer work on the large WPF projects I took part in. In a few days they were able to provide XAML files that made the application really appealing to the users. Without impacting business code.

## 3.2 Editors

Since there are two roles, there are two tools. Though you could use any of those tools in order to do all the work, each of them makes specific parts of the job faster and more convenient.

*Visual Studio* targets developers. Use it when adding controls, manually editing XAML, and writing the business logic.

*Blend for Visual Studio* targets designers. It is used when changing the appearance of controls and creating animations.

> *Blend for Visual Studio* is now installed together with Visual Studio. It was previously sold as a separate program, *Expression Blend*. When working with WPF

> with versions of Visual Studio that are older than Visual Studio 2013, you'll need to separately install Expression Blend if you need to use it.

## 3.3 Adding a control

There are two ways to add a control to a screen[1]:

1. drag and drop the control from the toolbox;
2. simply add an XML element in the XAML file.

In case you manually add the XML element, its position and size depends on the container. We'll talk about containers in the Layout chapter, but for now just be aware that the control will take all the screen size when added to a *Grid*, or remain at the top-left corner when added to a *Canvas*.

For instance, the following XAML code will display a *Button* control that spans the whole screen:

```
<Grid xmlns="...">
   <Button Content="Hello world" />
</Grid>
```

---

[1] All through this book, *screen* means window, or page, or user control. In fact, whatever container.

## 3.4 Simple controls

WPF provides relatively few controls. This is due to the fact that their appearance can be easily and completely revamped using pure XAML as we'll see in the Change a control's look chapter. Let's review the basic ones.

### Basic controls

There is almost no need to explain much about those controls. On the left, you can see their declaration in XAML; on the right, their *default*[2] appearance.

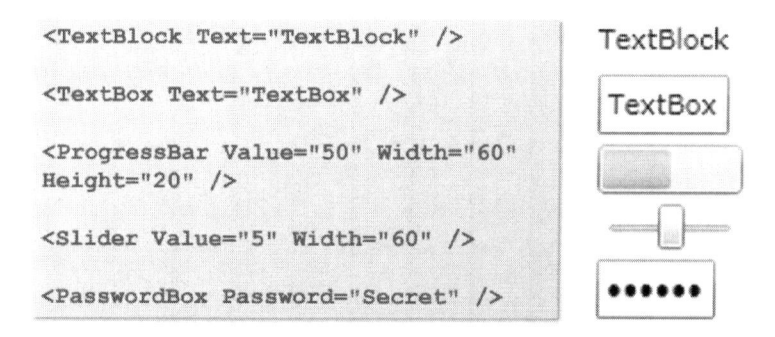

```
<TextBlock Text="TextBlock" />

<TextBox Text="TextBox" />

<ProgressBar Value="50" Width="60"
Height="20" />

<Slider Value="5" Width="60" />

<PasswordBox Password="Secret" />
```

TextBlock

TextBox

Those controls are symmetrical. While *TextBlock* and *TextBox* allow for a *string* to be displayed or input as their *Text* property, *ProgressBar* and *Slider* allow for a *double* to be displayed or input as their *Value* property.

Note that in order to display text, the *TextBlock* control should be preferred to the *Label* control. The *Label*

---
[2] Remember: a control's look can be easily changed using XAML.

control is a much more flexible content control, which means it can display much more than text. Since it can display anything, the *Label* control lacks properties like *TextWrapping* that enable long text to be wrapped, and can be found on the *TextBlock* control.

## Multimedia controls

The *Image* control displays, well, any picture, and the *MediaElement* displays movies. Both share a common resizing behavior:

- they resize their content to fit the size assigned to the control;
- they provide a *Stretch* property that enables you to specify how the content is resized.

The most interesting values of the *Stretch* property are:

- Uniform (default): Image is resized proportionally, leaving transparent margins on the sides as needed.
- Fill: Image is resized proportionally, filling up the whole space assigned to the *Image* control.

The following code will display a picture resized to be 50 tall (width is automatically computed since it is not provided) and a movie with the same characteristics.

```
<Image Source="fleurs.jpg" Height="50" />

<MediaElement Source="ic09.wmv" Height="50" />
```

> As stated earlier, sizes in WPF are not provided in pixels, since specifying pixels doesn't scale well when the screen resolution increases. Sizes are provided in *device-independent pixels*. If a screen is correctly calibrated, one device-independent pixel is about half a millimeter. This means that *50* represents around 2.5 centimeters on screen. This size would remain the same whatever the screen resolution you chose. Great news: that enables your application to perform well on nowadays' high screen resolutions.

## Drawing controls

The *Ellipse*, *Rectangle* and *Path* controls are basic shape drawing controls. They all share common properties:

- Fill: a *Brush* used to paint the inside of the control;
- Strike: a *Brush* used to paint the outline of the control;
- Stretch: how the control should resize its shape when resized, just like we saw for multimedia controls.

The *Path* control is very flexible: it enables you to provide a list of points and have them connected using segments or Bezier curves. Manually providing the points is too tedious so you have two options: draw the shape using *Blend for Visual Studio* or export the shape from a drawing or converter tool that generates XAML.

They are not container control so they can't have a child, but who cares? Should you need to add text to them, you can place a *TextBlock* over them, grouping both in a *Grid* control so they have the same size.

Apart from placing them anywhere on a screen, you can use them inside templates in order to give outstanding new appearances to existing controls. More about that a little later.

## Content controls

Content controls have a content that can be anything. For this, they expose a *Content* property. The following are content controls:

- Button
- Border
- ScrollViewer
- ViewBox

Here are some buttons. Again, their *default* appearance displayed on the right:

```
<Button Content="Un bouton" />

<ToggleButton Content="ToggleButton" />

<CheckBox Content="CheckBox" />

<RadioButton Content="RadioButton" />
```

Note that the *Content* property is assigned using a *Content* attribute. That works well with simple content. When you need to assign more complex content, you can provide a child element to your content control instead of using the *Content* attribute. Here are two examples:

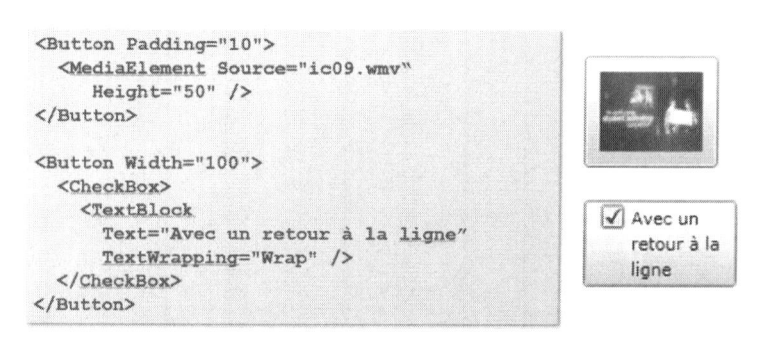

```
<Button Padding="10">
  <MediaElement Source="ic09.wmv"
    Height="50" />
</Button>

<Button Width="100">
  <CheckBox>
    <TextBlock
      Text="Avec un retour à la ligne"
      TextWrapping="Wrap" />
  </CheckBox>
</Button>
```

As I wrote, the content can be *anything*. Did you note how the example above adds a checkbox to a button? This simply wasn't possible with frameworks like Windows Forms because the *Button* control didn't have an *EnableCheckBox* property. Using WPF, you can simply combine controls in order to get the functionality you need. Plus you can also change their appearance, as we'll see later.

That gives you a great deal of flexibility. For instance, you may add scrolling around any control by just wrapping it inside a *ScrollViewer* control. Or a border to any control by wrapping it inside a *Border* control: don't look for a *Border* property on e.g. a *TextBlock* control: simply wrap it inside a *Border* control.

Here are examples of using the *Border* control and adding scrollbars to a movie using the *ScrollViewer* control.

```
<Border Background="Orange"
  CornerRadius="10" Padding="5">
    <Button Content="Un bouton" />
</Border>

<Border Background="Blue"
  CornerRadius="10,0,10,0" Padding="5">
    <Button Content="Un bouton" />
</Border>

<ScrollViewer Height="100" Width="100"
  HorizontalScrollBarVisibility="Auto">
    <MediaElement Source="ic09.wmv"
      Stretch="None" />
</ScrollViewer>
```

Now is time to introduce one of my preferred WPF controls to you: *ViewBox*. I love the *ViewBox* control because it shows the flexibility of WPF. It is able to resize any content just as if it were a picture, and the content remains usable. That means you can quickly have any kind of screen resized to the available width and height. It will come in very handy in control templates and many parts of your application.

Here is how the *ViewBox* control works:

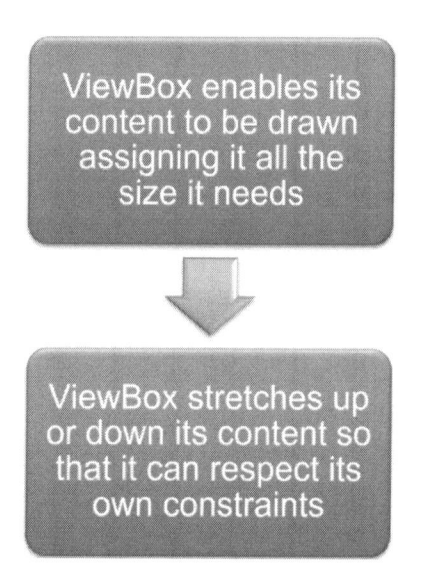

> ViewBox enables its content to be drawn assigning it all the size it needs
>
> ⬇
>
> ViewBox stretches up or down its content so that it can respect its own constraints

Now guess what? The *ViewBox* control has a *Strech* property that states how its content should be resized. And it behaves exactly like the *Strech* property of *Image* and *MediaElement* controls.

Let me show you simple uses of the *ViewBox* control together with their resulting display.

```
<Grid Height="60" Width="100" Background="LightBlue">
    <Button Content="A" />
</Grid>
```

In the above example, there is no *ViewBox* control. As we'll see later, a *Grid* control will stretch its content to fill in all of this space. So the *Button* control takes up all of the *Grid* control size.

```
<Grid Height="60" Width="100" Background="LightBlue">
    <Viewbox>
        <Button Content="A" />
    </Viewbox>
</Grid>
```

In that second example above, I just inserted a *ViewBox* control between the *Grid* control and the *Button* Control. The *Button* control is thus drawn using the size it needs (since there are no other constraints here, the size necessary to display its text), and then stretched up by the *ViewBox* control in order to fill all of the *Grid* control size. Note how the *Button* borders look thicker: all of the control was proportionally stretched.

Now, let me add just one attribute to the *ViewBox* control we used:

```
<Grid Height="60" Width="100" Background="LightBlue">
    <Viewbox Stretch="Fill">
        <Button Content="A" />
    </Viewbox>
</Grid>
```

Notice the result? The *Button* control is distorted.

Best part is that since *ViewBox* is a content control it can be used in order to resize a full screen. Suppose you have the following screen:

```
<Grid xmlns="...">
  <Button Content="Hello world" ... />
  <ListBox ... />
  <DataGrid ... />
</Grid>
```

You can have that whole screen resize to any dimension

just adding a *ViewBox* control:

```
<ViewBox xmlns="...">
  <Grid>
    <Button Content="Hello world" ... />
    <ListBox ... />
    <DataGrid ... />
  </Grid>
</ViewBox>
```

This method is quick to implement but has its drawbacks: it resizes all of the content. If you want some more complex resizing like providing more space to the ListBox control, you should use layout controls.

## 3.5 Navigation

Users are now used to navigating inside an application. Going back to the previous screen, and back again in the history, is likely to be part of your application's requirements. WPF comes in with a navigation framework that may come handy, though you are free to use another one.

When using WPF navigation system, screens are Pages, and they are displayed within a single *Frame* control. Think of the *Frame* control as a Web browser and of the Pages as Web pages.

Pages are XAML files, and you can consider them just like Windows except they have no borders or window-related properties. They are a subclass of user controls, so you could also think of them as user controls. Anyway, in order to create a page you just add a *Page* element using Visual Studio, and get roughly the following XAML:

```
<Page x:Class="..." Title="...">
  <Grid>
      ...
  </Grid>
<Page>
```

You will create as many pages as your application needs screens, and then you'll add a *Frame* control that will serve as the page browser. A natural place to put the *Frame* control is the *MainWindow.xaml* window that has been created by default. Next, you tell the *Frame* control which page to display using the *Source* property.

You get something like that (probably inside *MainWindow.xaml*):

```
<Frame Source="/Welcome.xaml">
<Frame>
```

⚠️ Don't forget the "/" in front of the page name.

This code would display the Welcome page. Now, you need a way for the user to move from one page to another. You can do so using XAML or C#.

**Navigate to another page using code-behind**

```
NavigationService.Navigate(
  new Uri("/Payment.xaml", UriKind.Relative)
);
```

**Link to another page using XAML**

```
<Label>
  <Hyperlink NavigateUri="/Payment.xaml">
    Pay now
  </Hyperlink>
</Label>
```

# 3.6 It's your turn to code: do-it-yourself

Now is your turn to grab the keyboard and code away. Oh, just let me explain you how that works, in case you're not familiar with my *Learn collection* books.

## About exercises in this book

All of the exercises are linked together: you're going to build a small e-commerce application. You'll allow users to browse through your products, add them to their basket, and you'll also create a full back-end where the site administrators will be able to list, create, modify, and delete products.

## In case you get stuck

You should be able to solve the exercise all by yourself. If you get stuck or don't have a computer at hand (or you don't have the prerequisites for that book, which is fine with me!), no problem. I'll provide the solution for all of the exercises in this book, right after each of them.

## 3.7 Exercise - Create the application and contact page

Create a new WPF application named *BikeShop*.

Add a new page named *Contact.xaml* to the application.

Add two *TextBox* controls and two *TextBlock* controls to the *Contact* page so that a user can input a message.

Make sure that the *Contact* page is displayed by default on the *MainWindow.xaml* screen

Your application should look like the following:

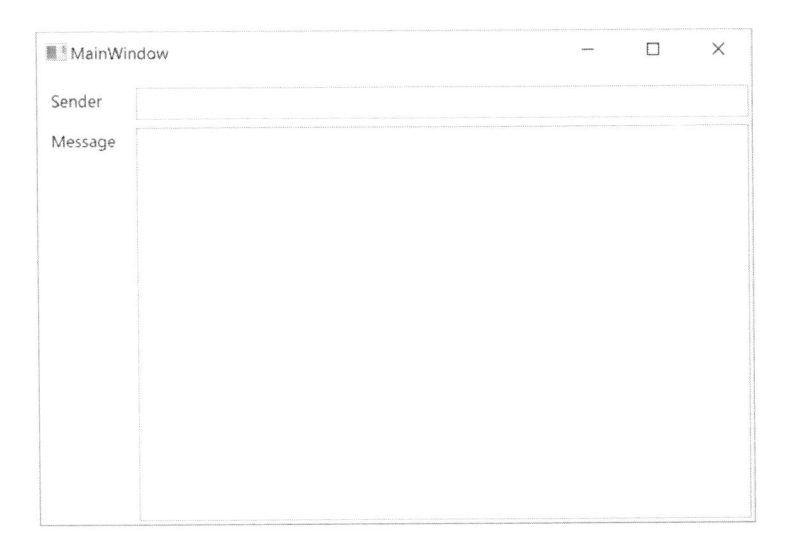

[MainWindow mockup with "Sender" text field and "Message" text area]

I know, it's basic, but you need to learn some more things before you can do more.

Beginner badge unlocked: let's proceed to the next level.

## 3.8 Exercise solution

- Start Visual Studio.
- Click on the *File / New / Project…* menu entry.
- In the *New Project* dialog box, select the *WPF Application* template making sure that you select *Templates / Visual C# / Windows* on the left-hand side. In the *Name* zone at the bottom, type "BikeShop". Click the *OK* button.
- Open the *Solution Explorer* clicking on the *View / Solution Explorer* menu entry.

- In the *Solution Explorer*, right-click the project (not the solution), and select *Add / Page* from the context menu.
- In the *Add New Item* dialog box, look for the *Name* zone at the bottom, and type "Contact". Click the *Add* button.
- Open the *Toolbox* clicking on the *View / Toolbox* menu entry.
- Drag and drop two *TextBlock* controls and two *TextBox* controls from the toolbox to the design surface. Position them and resize them so that the screen looks as expected.
- Make sure that the *Properties* window is displayed clicking on the *View / Properties Window* menu entry.
- Click the first *TextBlock* control and change its *Text* property to *Sender*.
- Click the second *TextBlock* control and change its *Text* property to *Message*.
- Click the first *TextBox* control and change its *Text* property to be an empty string.
- Click the second *TextBox* control and change its *Text* property to be an empty string.
- In the *Solution Explorer*, double-click the *MainWindow.xaml* file.
- Inside the *Grid* element, add a *Frame* element. The *MainWindow.xaml* code should look like this:

```
<Window ...>
  <Grid>
    <Frame Source="/Contact.xaml" />
  </Grid>
</Window>
```

- Run the application (click on the *Debug / Start Debugging* menu entry).
- Close the application.

## 3.9 Understanding XAML

Now comes a central part: understanding XAML from a developer point of view. If you feel that this part is too theoretical, you can safely skip it. Many WPF developers don't have that level of XAML understanding and use internet forums to compensate for that lack. However, if you keep on and read that part, you'll gain superpowers when developing WPF applications.

Still here? Good, buckle-up your seatbelt and let's go!

### XAML namespaces

The page you just created has several *xmlns* attributes applied to the root element. Basically, XAML files will look like this:

```
<StackPanel
  xmlns="http://schemas.microsoft.com/winfx/2006/xaml\
/presentation"
  xmlns:x="http://schemas.microsoft.com/winfx/2006/xa\
ml">
  <Button x:Name="someButton">Hello</Button>
</StackPanel>
```

The *xmlns* attributes are an XML concept. They declare the use of an XML namespace, just like the C# *using* keyword does for C# code. Their value is an URL. Even though the URLs begin with "http://", there is no guarantee that pointing a browser to the URL will display anything: XML uses URLs only as a way to ensure that the namespaces are unique across different XML documents.

When a *xmlns* attribute is added to an element, it means that this element and its children are in fact prefixed by default with the corresponding URL. So in my example above, the *StackPanel* element actually is:

http://schemas..../presentation:StackPanel.

Likewise, an *xmlns:something* attribute means that any element that is prefixed with *something* is in fact prefixed by the corresponding URL. So in my example above, the *x:Name* attribute is in fact:

http://schemas..../xaml:Name.

There will be several *xmlns:something* attributes in your XAML files, corresponding to various XML namespaces, but the basic ones for WPF are:

**http://schemas.microsoft.com/winfx/2006/xaml/presentation**

WPF controls. In fact, it is mapped to the .NET WPF namespaces: System.Windows, System.Windows.Controls, System.Windows.Media.Media3D, …

**http://schemas.microsoft.com/winfx/2006/xaml**

XAML keywords. For instance, the *x:Name* attribute is mapped to this namespace because it can be used within any XAML file, not just WPF-related XAML files.

## Object creation

XAML is simply one more .NET language. Even though it is used as a simple appearance description tool, its syntax hides a powerful language. In fact, it is an easy way to create objects. For instance, those two syntaxes are equivalent:

**Creating an object in C#**
```
new Car();
```

**Creating an object in XAML**
```
<Car />
```

In those examples, *Car* can be any class. Since no prefix means "WPF controls", and there is no *Car* control in WPF, it will fail. But we can map XAML namespaces to any .NET namespace including our own, using the following XAML syntax:

```
xmlns:anything="namespace:some;assembly:MyAssembly"
```

In that case, the "assembly:MyAssembly" part is optional, and used only when the namespace is part of a project different from the XAML file.

Now, suppose we declare a *Car* class for real:

```
namespace BusinessLogic
{
  public class Car
  {
    public double Speed { get; set; }
    public Color Color { get; set; }
  }
}
```

Then we could use it with any of the two syntaxes. The C# syntax you know, and the XAML one we just described:

**Creating an object in C#**

```
using BusinessLogic;

new Car();
```

**Creating an object in XAML**

```
<Label xmlns:bl="clr-namespace:BusinessLogic">
  <bl:Car />
</Label>
```

## Properties definition

Got it? XAML is a .NET language. Now let's take things further. We can easily assign values to the properties of the objects we create in XAML. Here are again two equivalent codes:

**Creating an object and assigning properties in C#**

```
using BusinessLogic;

var c = new Car();
c.Speed = 100;
c.Color = Colors.Red;
```

**Creating an object and assigning properties in XAML**

```
<Label xmlns:bl="namespace:BusinessLogic">
  <bl:Car Speed="100" Color="Red" />
</Label>
```

Easy: XML attributes map to the properties of an object. There is an automatic translation from the strings you provide to the real .NET types like double or enumerations.

You can even pass in complex objects as property values, but the syntax is more verbose. Suppose the *Car* and *Human* classes are defined as such:

```
namespace BusinessLogic
{
  public class Human
  {
    public string FirstName { get; set; }
    public bool HasDrivingLicense { get; set; }
  }

  public class Car
  {
    public double Speed { get; set; }
    public Color { get; set; }
    public Human Driver { get; set; }
  }
}
```

The two following codes would be equivalent:

**Creating an object and assigning properties in C#**

```csharp
using BusinessLogic;

var h = new Human();
h.FirstName = "Nick";
h.HasDrivingLicense = true;

var c = new Car();
c.Color = Colors.Red;
c.Driver = h;
```

**Creating an object and assigning properties in XAML**

```xml
<Label xmlns:bl="namespace:BusinessLogic">
  <bl:Car Color="Red">
    <bl:Car.Driver>
      <bl:Human FirstName="Nick"
                HasDrivingLicense="true" />
    </bl:Car.Driver>
  </bl:Car>
</Label>
```

The syntax gets a little bit more complex, but there really is no other way. I'd love to be able to write something along those lines:

**Invalid syntax**

```
<bl:Car
  Color="Red"
  Driver="bl:Human FirstName=Nick, HasDrivingLicense=\
true">
</bl:Car>
```

However XAML defines such a syntax only for known classes like the *Binding* class. So just get used to the sub-element syntax.

## Naming

When you want to manipulate in the code-behind an object you declared in the XAML file, or simply want some XAML element to reference another XAML element, you can add a *x:Name* attribute. For instance:

**SomeScreen.xaml**

```
<bl:Car x:Name="myCar" Speed="100" Color="Red" />
```

**SomeScreen.xaml.cs**

```
public partial class SomeScreen : Page
{
  public SomeScreen()
  {
    InitializeComponent();
    myCar.Color = Color.Blue;
  }
}
```

When displayed, *SomeScreen* will display a blue car.

> The call to InitializeComponent() in a code-behind means "do what the XAML states". It is obviously placed by default in the screen constructor by Visual Studio.

When practicing XAML you'll notice this oddity: you can both use *x:Name* or *Name* attribute on XAML controls. In fact, they have the same meaning. So What's the difference, you ask? To make a long story short, *x:Name* can always be used, while the shorter *Name* can only be used on WPF controls and when using WPF versions 3.5 or higher.

## 3.10 Events

WPF controls declare events, and just like properties they are available as attributes in XAML. You simply provide code-behind method names to the attributes. So the following code would handle the *Click* event of a button using code-behind:

SomeScreen.xaml

```
<Button Click="Greet" />
```

SomeScreen.xaml.cs

```
private void Greet(object sender, RoutedEventArgs e)
{
    MessageBox.Show("Hello");
}
```

> Visual Studio can generate the XAML and C# code associated with event handling. In the *Properties* window, when a control is selected, click the *Event handlers* button at the top-right. Then double-click in the empty zone next to an event name, and you're done. As a shortcut, if you just want to handle the "default" event for a control, double-click it on the design surface.

Events travel up (mostly) or down (sometimes) the control tree. What we call control tree is the XML hierarchy in the XAML file.

Suppose we write the following XAML:

```
<Grid MouseLeftButtonDown="SaySomething">
  <Button MouseLeftButtonDown="SayHello" />
  <Button MouseLeftButtonDown="SayGoodbye" />
</Grid>
```

When the first button is clicked, the *SayHello* and *SaySomething* methods will both be invoked. When the second button is clicked, the *SayGoodbye* and *SaySomething* methods will both be invoked[3].

> WPF defines *bubble* and *tunnel* event types. Most events are *bubble* type, which means they travel up the control tree, so the *SayHello* method is invoked before the *SaySomething* one. Events whose name begins with "Preview" are *tunnel* type.

---

[3] My younger son Nicolas' favorite song at the moment is *Hello goodbye* from the Beatles. Those method names are for him. :-)

## 3.11 Exercise - Create the menu page

Add a new page named *Menu.xaml* to the application and make sure that it is displayed by default on the *MainWindow.xaml* screen instead of the *Contact* page.

Add three *Button* controls and one *TextBlock control* to the *Menu* page.

When the last *Button* control is clicked, make sure that the application navigates to the *Contact* page.

Your application should look like the following when started:

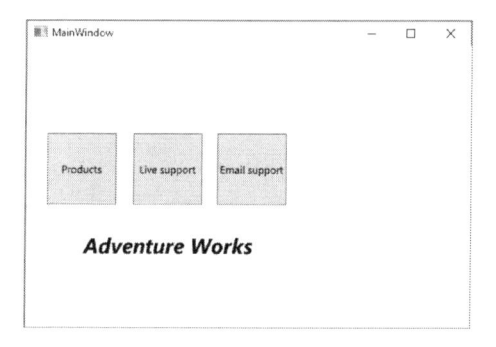

## 3.12 Exercise solution

- Switch to Visual Studio.

- Open the *Solution Explorer* clicking on the *View / Solution Explorer* menu entry.
- In the *Solution Explorer*, right-click the project (not the solution), and select *Add / Page* from the context menu.
- In the *Add New Item* dialog box, look for the *Name* zone at the bottom, and type "Menu". Click the *Add* button.
- Open the *Toolbox* clicking on the *View / Toolbox* menu entry.
- Drag and drop three *Button* controls and one *TextBlock* control from the toolbox to the design surface. Position them and resize them so that the screen looks as expected.
- Make sure that the *Properties* window is displayed clicking on the *View / Properties Window* menu entry.
- Click the first *Button* control and change its *Content* property to *Products*.
- Click the second *Button* control and change its *Content* property to *Live support*.
- Click the third *Button* control and change its *Content* property to *Email support*.
- Click the *TextBlock* control and change its *Text* property to *Adventure Works*.
- Double-click the button that reads "Email support". This adds a *Click* attribute to the XAML, an event handler to the code-behind, and opens the code-behind.
- Add the following code to the created event handler:

```
private void button_Click(object sender,
  RoutedEventArgs e)
{
  NavigationService.Navigate(
    new Uri("/Contact.xaml", UriKind.Relative)
  );
}
```

- In the *Solution Explorer*, double-click the *MainWindow.xaml* file.
- Change the *Source* attribute of the *Frame* element to be:

```
<Frame Source="/Menu.xaml" />
```

- Run the application (click on the *Debug / Start Debugging* menu entry).
- Click on the "Email support" button. Check that the *Contact* page is displayed.
- Navigate back to the menu page using the button that appeared in the top-left corner.
- Close the application.

## 3.13 Layout

### Why our screens don't resize

If you resize our application's window, you'll notice that the controls don't move. They remain where they are, which means any extra space is lost when the window is resized larger, and parts of the controls are hidden when the windows is made smaller. You sure want to avoid that. Moreover, wouldn't it be nice if the controls were centered on our menu page?

Up to now, we've been adding controls to our screens using drag and drop from the *Toolbox* to the design surface. Visual Studio converts those drag and drop gestures into control properties: *Width*, *Height*, plus *Left* and *Top* (when the root control is a *Canvas*) or *HorizontalAlignment* and *VerticalAlignment* (when the root control is a *Grid*). Those properties assign the controls' location and size, which is why we see fixed controls on our screens.

Fear not: it's quite easy to get controls to flow around the screen when it is resized. All you need to do is use *Panel* controls and understand how size is allocated to controls in a WPF application. Which is exactly what comes next.

## Size allocation

WPF goes through the following process in order to compute the final width of a control. Needless to say that the same process is repeated in order to compute the height.

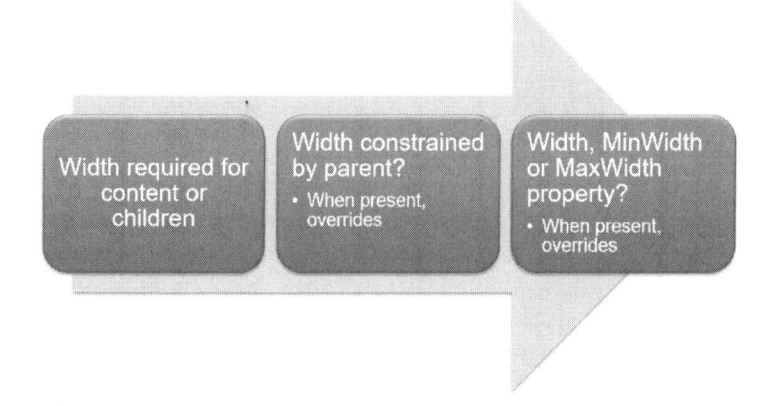

[Diagram: Arrow flow showing three stages:
1. Width required for content or children
2. Width constrained by parent? • When present, overrides
3. Width, MinWidth or MaxWidth property? • When present, overrides]

> The *Width* property is in fact just the *desired* width. Should you want to know the actual width that was assigned to a control at runtime, just use the *ActualWidth* property of the control.

As you can see from the schema above, first WPF queries for the size required by the control's children, then the one constrained by its parent, and eventually checks for a *Width*, *MinWidth* or *MaxWidth* property on the control itself. The parent constrained size will supersede the children required size, then the *Width* properties will supersede those values.

Suppose we have the following code:

```
<Canvas Width="50" Height="50" Background="Orange">
  <Button Content="Hello world" Margin="5" />
</Canvas>
```

A *Canvas* control doesn't constrain its children size (as we'll see shortly) and there is no *Width* property on the *Button* control, so the *Button* control will be assigned the size that is needed in order to display the "Hello world" text in full.

This is what the result looks like:

Now, consider the following code:

```
<Grid Width="50" Height="50" Background="Orange">
  <Button Content="Hello world" Margin="5" />
</Grid>
```

Since the *Grid* control constrains its children's size (again, we'll see that shortly), the *Button* control will be assigned the width of the *Grid* control and its text will be truncated. This is what the result looks like:

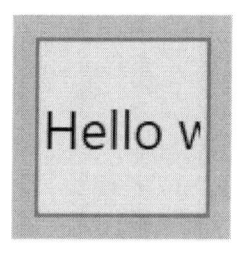

## Panel controls

Panel controls are used for two reasons:

- display several controls where only one control is allowed (inside a *Button* control, and event inside a *Page* or *Window*);
- layout the controls according to the available size.

The layout part is a very interesting aspect of the panel controls. When used widely, they enable your application screens to adapt to the available screen estate (call this *responsive design* if you want to sound hype).

Ladies and gentlemen, please let me introduce you to my beloved panel controls.

## Canvas

The *Canvas* panel allows you to place controls providing their coordinates. It doesn't coerce any size on the controls, which means that the controls are free to state their size or have it coerced by their own children. The position of its inner controls is declared using the *Canvas.Left* and *Canvas.Top* properties on each of its inner controls.

> *Canvas.Left* and *Canvas.Top* are *attached* properties. They don't exist as such on each control, rather the *Canvas* control declares *Left* and *Right* properties stating that they can be attached to other controls. This is an almost magic feature of *dependency properties* that we'll see later.

Here is an sample *Canvas* use:

```
<Canvas>
    <Button Canvas.Top="0" Canvas.Left="0">A</Button>
    <Button Canvas.Top="25" Canvas.Left="0">B</Button>
    <Button Canvas.Top="25" Canvas.Left="25">C</Button>
    <Button Canvas.Top="0" Canvas.Left="50">D</Button>
</Canvas>
```

The result would look like:

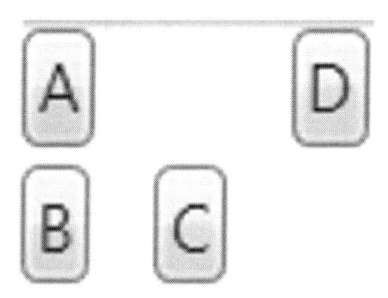

Typing the XAML necessary to place controls on a Canvas is tedious, so don't do it: simply use the design view in Visual Studio to drag and drop the child controls from the toolbox: their *Canvas.Left*, *Canvas.Top*, *Width* and *Height* properties will be assigned automatically.

## StackPanel

A basic panel that comes in very handy when you're manually editing your XAML. On the other hand using a *StackPanel* from the design view is cumbersome. It simply stacks controls from the bottom to the top, allocating full width to each of them.

That can be changed using the *Orientation* control of the *StackPanel* control. Set it to *Horizontal* and its children will flow from left to right filling the whole height. Furthermore, you can use *HorizontalAlignment* and *VerticalAlignment* properties on the controls in order to change the fact that they use full width or height.

Here are sample *StackPanel* uses and their results:

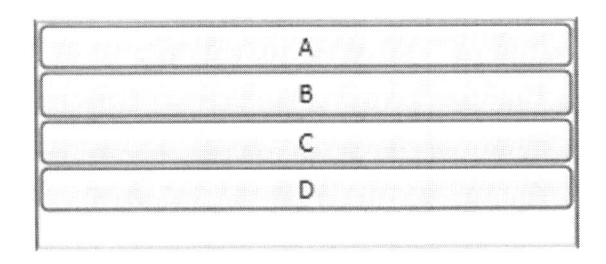

```xml
<StackPanel Orientation="Vertical">
  <Button>A</Button>
  <Button>B</Button>
  <Button>C</Button>
  <Button>D</Button>
</StackPanel>
```

```xml
<StackPanel Orientation="Horizontal">
  <Button>A</Button>
  <Button>B</Button>
  <Button>C</Button>
  <Button>D</Button>
</StackPanel>
```

## DockPanel

Another panel which is simple to use when manually editing your XAML, and cumbersome from the design view. It allows you to quickly get screen layouts like most desktop applications.

All you have to do is use the attached *DockPanel.Dock* attached properties on the controls you place incide the *DockPanel*.

Here is a sample *DockPanel* use and its result:

```
<DockPanel>
  <Button DockPanel.Dock="Left">
    Left
  </Button>
  <Button DockPanel.Dock="Right">
    Right
  </Button>
  <Button DockPanel.Dock="Top">
    Top
  </Button>
  <Button>Takes what's left</Button>
</DockPanel>
```

```
┌─────────────────────────────┐
│         Top                 │
├────┬───────────────────┬────┤
│Left│                   │Right│
│    │  Takes what's left│    │
│    │                   │    │
└────┴───────────────────┴────┘
```

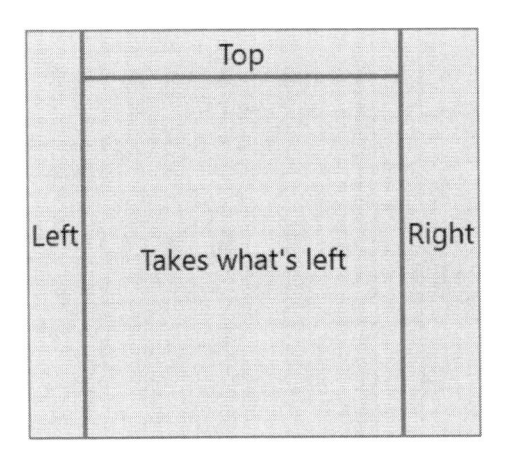

## WrapPanel

Simple to use when manually editing your XAML, it simply lets its controls flow from left to right, going back to the right when all the width has been used. Much like a word processor with your text.

## UniformGrid

Great for laying out an input UI in no time when manually editing your XAML.

Mind you, this control is quite smart: it automatically computes the amount of lines and columns it needs for your controls. For instance, if the *UniformGrid* control has 9 children it will accomodate them using 3 lines and 3 columns.

You can also constrain it using its *Rows* or *columns* properties. For instance, if the *UniformGrid* control has

9 children and you provide a value of 2 for its *Columns* property, it will accomodate the controls using 5 lines and 2 columns.

The only real trouble with the *UniformGrid* control is that all rows and columns are created with equal width and height. Which makes it only suitable for prototyping.

Here is a sample *DockPanel* use and its result:

```
<UniformGrid>
  <Label>Name</Label>
  <TextBox Width="70" />
  <Label>Age</Label>
  <ComboBox />
</UniformGrid>
```

### Grid

Mind you, this is the most polyvalent control for resizable layouts. With power comes complexity: you don't want to use it when manually editing your XAML since it needs quite a bunch of XAML. But the design view in Visual Studio or Blend handles it perfectly right.

Here's a basic layout using a *Grid* control and how it appears:

```
<Grid Width="200" Height="100">
  <Grid.ColumnDefinitions>
    <ColumnDefinition />
    <ColumnDefinition />
  </Grid.ColumnDefinitions>
  <Grid.RowDefinitions>
    <RowDefinition />
    <RowDefinition />
  </Grid.RowDefinitions>
  <Button Grid.Row="0"
          Grid.Column="0">Button A</Button>
  <Button Grid.Row="1"
          Grid.Column="0">Button B</Button>
  <Button Grid.Row="1"
          Grid.Column="1">Button C</Button>
  <Button Grid.Row="0"
          Grid.Column="1">Button D</Button>
</Grid>
```

|  |  |
|---|---|
| Button A | Button D |
| Button B | Button C |

Controls laid out using a *Grid* behave according to the following rules:

- A control fills up the whole cell it belongs to;
- Controls that belong to the same cell appear on top of each other;
- A control can fill up several columns or rows using the attached properties *Grid.RowSpan* and *Grid.ColumnSpan*.

Note how rows and columns are defined using the *RowDefinitions* and *ColumnDefinitions* properties of the *Grid*. There can be as many definitions as necessary.

When nothing is stated, the available width (or height) is equally divided between all of the defined columns (or rows). However, you can change that behavior using the *Width* property on the column definitions (or *Height* property of the rows definitions).

There are three possible values for the *Width* and *Height* properties:

- A fixed number: the column/row will be assigned that amount of pixels;
- *Auto*: the column/row will adapt its size to its contents;
- A star, or a number followed by stars: the column/row will be assigned a size proportional to the remaining width/height. Let me explain.

Consider the following example:

```
<Grid.ColumnDefinitions>
  <ColumnDefinition Width="30" />
  <ColumnDefinition Width="*" />
  <ColumnDefinition Width="2*" />
</Grid.ColumnDefinitions>
```

The first column is assigned a fixed size. Then the remaining width is assigned to the two starred columns. The second column has one star, and the third two stars. The sum of all defined stars is three, so the second column is assigned 1/3 of the width and the third, 2/3 of the width.

> \* and 1\* are fully equivalent.

### Summary of panel controls

Here is a list of the panel controls we saw. Some of them are better suited for manual XAML writing since they require little XAML, while others are better suited for the Visual Studio design surface since they require a bunch of XAML.

For instance, when manually editting XAML I would prefer using a *StackPanel* control rather than a *Grid* control.

| Control | Coerces size | Easier using |
| --- | --- | --- |
| Canvas | No | Design view |
| DockPanel | Yes | XAML |
| Grid | Yes | Design view |
| StackPanel | Yes | XAML |
| UniformGrid | Yes | XAML |
| WrapPanel | Yes | XAML |

All in all, when using the Visual Studio design view on a screen, you should prefer *Canvas* (for fixed layouts) and *Grid* (for resize-able layouts) controls.

## 3.14 List controls

That chapter wouldn't be complete if I didn't mention the list controls. I'll do that quickly for now, since most of the time their elements won't be defined using XAML but rather they will be bound to data object collections. Which we'll see in the Displaying collections using list controls chapter.

Another common point about those list controls is that you can provide a template that changes the looks of the control but also an item template that will change how each item is displayed (we'll learn about that in the Customizing list controls chapter). Which means two things:

- the appearance shown below is the *default* appearance, easily changed;
- you should focus on the required behavior, not appearance, for choosing controls.

## Selection controls

*ListBox* allows for the selection of one or more items, and can display several items at a time. *ComboBox* allows for the selection of one item and has two display modes: one where the selected element is shown, and one where the available elements are shown.

```
<ListBox Height="100">
  <Label>Element 1</Label>
  <Label>Element 2</Label>
  <GroupBox Header="Element 3">
    With some content, it's funnier
  </GroupBox>
</ListBox>
```

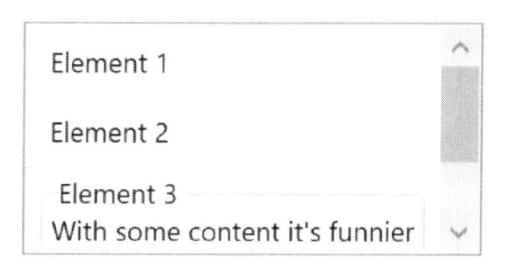

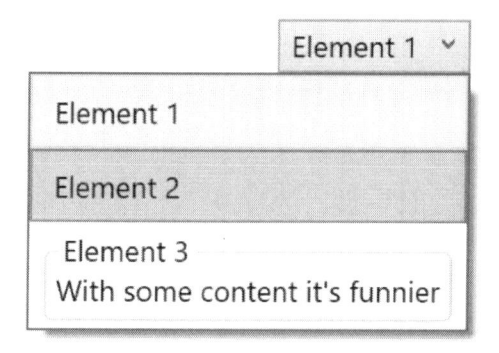

```
<ComboBox>
  <Label>Element 1</Label>
  <Label>Element 2</Label>
  <GroupBox Header="Element 3">
    With some content it's funnier
  </GroupBox>
</ComboBox>
```

A *TabControl* is mostly the same as a *ComboBox* except that its elements can have a header (always shown) and a content. Which is materialized using *TabItem* elements as child controls.

## 3.15 Exercise - Create the discussion page

Add a new page named *Discussion.xaml* to the application and make sure that it is displayed when the user clicks the chat button of the menu page.

Add a *ListBox* control that will later display the messages exchanged between the client support and user. Add *TextBox* and *Button* controls that will later allow the user to type and send her messages.

Your page should look like that:

[MainWindow mockup showing an empty ListBox area, a "Type your message here" TextBox, and a "Send" Button]

> Make sure that the page handles resizes. When resized, the *ListBox* control should grow (width and height), the *Button* control should remain on the right and the *TextBox* control's width should grow.
>
> This is how your page should resize:

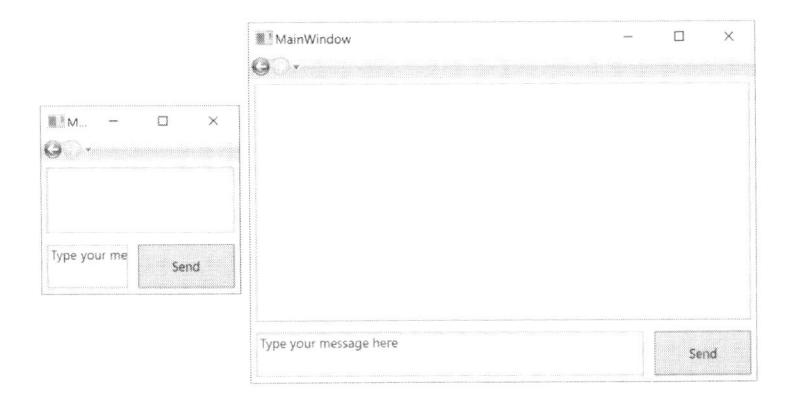

## 3.16 Exercise solution

- Switch to Visual Studio.
- Open the *Solution Explorer* clicking on the *View / Solution Explorer* menu entry.
- In the *Solution Explorer*, right-click the project (not the solution), and select *Add / Page* from the context menu.
- In the *Add New Item* dialog box, look for the *Name* zone at the bottom, and type "Discussion". Click the *Add* button.
- In the *Solution Explorer*, double-click the *Menu.xaml* file.
- Double-click the button that reads "Live support". This adds a *Click* attribute to the XAML, an event handler to the code-behind, and opens the code-behind.
- Add the following code to the created event handler:

# Creating a WPF application

```
private void button1_Click(object sender,
  RoutedEventArgs e)
{
  NavigationService.Navigate(
    new Uri("/Discussion.xaml", UriKind.Relative)
  );
}
```

- In the *Solution Explorer*, double-click the *Discussion.xaml* file. Add the following XAML code to the page:

```
<Grid>
  <Grid.ColumnDefinitions>
    <ColumnDefinition Width="*" />
    <ColumnDefinition Width="100" />
  </Grid.ColumnDefinitions>
  <Grid.RowDefinitions>
    <RowDefinition Height="*" />
    <RowDefinition Height="50" />
  </Grid.RowDefinitions>
  <ListBox Grid.ColumnSpan="2"
           Margin="5" />
  <Button Grid.Row="1"
          Grid.Column="1"
          Margin="5"
          Content="Send" />
  <TextBox Grid.Row="1"
           Margin="5"
```

```
              Text="Type your message here" />
</Grid>
```

- Run the application (click on the *Debug / Start Debugging* menu entry).
- Click on the "Live support" button. Check that the *Discussion* page is displayed and resizes as expected.
- Close the application.

# 4. Managing data in a WPF application

## 4.1 Data binding

Almost all of the applications we create today are data centric. Which means they get data from some data store (database, file system, cloud, …), display it to the user, allow the user to make changes, and send the data updates to the data store. At a point in time, you have in-memory data and the user interface should be synchronized.

Now, there are two ways to go about that: write a bunch of code, or be lazy. WPF allows you to go for the second one and be lazy. Which means writing very little code in order to enable your UI to remain synchronized with your data. Not only does this mean faster application creation, it also means much fewer work during application maintenance.

When you look at a data-centric application, there are controls that display data. Which means you get a variable to be assigned to a control's property; when the user interacts with the control the property changes, and you handle an event and write the modified data to the original variable. WPF allows you to avoid all of that code

70        Managing data in a WPF application

and write just a few XAML characters instead using **data binding**.

Let's suppose you want to display the speed of a car. Here is how WPF goes about it:

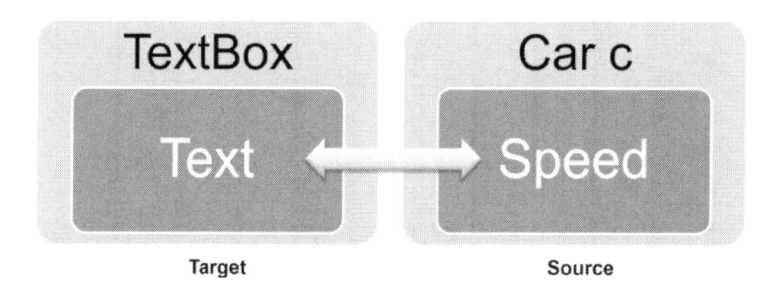

```
      TextBox              Car c
    ┌─────────┐         ┌─────────┐
    │  Text   │ ◄─────► │  Speed  │
    └─────────┘         └─────────┘
      Target              Source
```

The *Text* property will be literally *connected* to the value of the *Speed* property of your data object, which means the *Speed* property will be initially assigned to the *Text* property of the *TextBox* control, and any change to the *Text* property (the user types in some value, for instance) will be assigned to the *Speed* property of your data object.

In order to get all of that, you just have one XAML line to write:

`<TextBox Text="{Binding Speed, ElementName=c}" />`

Easy, right? You already knew about the `<TextBox Text="..." />` syntax, now all you need to understand is this data binding syntax that states how the *Text* property should be connected to the *Speed* property.

It's quite simple in fact: after the *Binding* keyword you write the name of the data object property you want to connect to, and then you may state how the data object should be located. Here, we used the *ElementName* syntax stating that the data object is a named element.

The most simple way to define a data binding is:

```
<TextBox Text="{Binding Speed}" />
```

In that case, the source data object is looked for in the current data context (see DataContext). It is equivalent to the following, explicit syntax, which you may see since it is generally used by code generators:

```
<TextBox Text="{Binding Path=Speed}" />
```

In case you omit the Path= syntax, the path property must be the first one to appear, like in the example above.

There are tons of other properties you can use inside a binding. In my first example you could see the use of the ElementName property, which states that the source data object is another control that has a x:Name property. This may be useful, for instance when you quickly want to show or hide a panel according to a checkbox's checked state.

Another property you may encounter quite often is the one where you state that the source data object is defined as a resource:

```
<TextBox Text="{Binding Source={StaticResource someLi\
st}, Path=Height}" />
```

> If you use the strange example above, the *someList* control's height would really be displayed by the *TextBox* control, and typing a new value inside the *TextBox* control would change the height of the *someList* control. Powerful syntax, isn't it?

Please bear with me: I have a few more things to state about data binding.

## Binding examples

Just look at the following example:

```
<StackPanel>
  <Slider Maximum="100"
          Value="10"
          x:Name="slider" />
  <ProgressBar
    Value="{Binding Value, ElementName=slider}" />
  <TextBox
    Text="{Binding Value, ElementName=slider}" />
</StackPanel>
```

This results in a screen where all controls are connected: move the slider and the *ProgressBar* and *TextBox* will update to reflect the new value. Type a value in the *TextBox* and the other controls will update. Type a text in the *TextBox* and its border will turn red when it loses focus in order to show that the value cannot be converted to a number. Type a value greater than 100 and it will be set back to 100.

That's a bunch of things done magically for you using just a few lines of XAML, right? Think about how many lines of C# would be required in order to get the same behavior (convert from string to double, handle and report errors, synchronize all three controls) if writing code-behind (whether in WPF, Windows Form or another UI technology). How many would you need? 30 lines? Plus another benefit is that you can copy-paste this XAML to any screen and it will still work, while code-behind would need you to copy the controls *and* C# code.

Now let's have a look at another example:

```
<Window
  Background="{Binding Text, ElementName=color}">
  <TextBox Text="Yellow"
           x:Name="color" />
</Window>
```

You guessed it: the window's background appears yellow, and you can type any valid color value in the TextBox. The WPF binding system automatically converts the string value from the *Text* property to a *Brush* instance (which is the type of the *Background* property). Wow! Now just think for a moment about how much time you're going to save using this kind of productivity for your data centric applications.

## Binding Mode

By default, the data binding mode depends on the control property you bind to. For controls that allow user input it will be *TwoWay*, for others it will be *OneWay*. The possible values are:

| Mode | Update on target change | value change |
|---|---|---|
| TwoWay | Yes | Yes |
| OneWay | No | Yes |
| OneWayToSource | Yes | No |
| OneTime | No | No |

> *OneWayToSource* and *OneTime* are scarcely used.

In case the default binding option doesn't suit you, you can override it using the data binding *Mode* property:

```
{Binding Path=Speed, Mode=TwoWay}
```

## Binding errors

Data binding in WPF applications is a real time saver during development and maintenance thanks to its very concise syntax. However, with great power come great responsibility: you may find yourself overlooking an error a little too quickly.

A binding error results in no unhandled exception at runtime, so it's easy to miss it. Sometimes, that's what you want: a null or incorrect value will simply be ignored, which is usually part of the application requirements. But other errors result in the application silently malfunctioning. For instance, an error in the *Path* property or an incompatible type (e.g. an object value bound to an *int* property).

By default, if you want to see those errors, you should:

- Run the application in *Debug* mode;
- Manually go through the screens;
- Look at the debug output window in Visual Studio for lines that start with "System.Data Error".

Such lines report all of the information about binding errors that are needed for troubleshooting.

## 4.2 DataContext

In a data centric application's screen, most controls that are visually grouped together take their data from the same data object. How about taking this into account in order to simplify the XAML we write for a binding?

DRY[1] is a good coding practice and that's exactly what DataContext is about.

When you don't specify a source data object in a binding (using *ElementName*, *Source* or the likes), the source is assumed to be the current data context. Let's look at an example before I explain the inner workings:

```
<StackPanel DataContext="...">
  <TextBox Text="{Binding Name}" />
  <Label Content="{Binding SSN}" />
</StackPanel>
```

In that example I could also omit the `DataContext="..."` part and assign it from the code-behind, for instance writing:

```
this.DataContext = ... ;
```

Practically, every control has a *DataContext* property which is typed as *object*: that means you can assign any object type to it. When a binding expression mentions no source, the source is assumed to be the control's *DataContext* property. What makes it Powerful is that when the *DataContext* is not assigned (*null* default value), the *DataContext* of the parent control is used (and so on, in case that *DataContext* is also missing).

---

[1] Don't Repeat Yourself

> DataContext is one of the great XAML time savers that aren't used enough by XAML developers. Learn to use it, and you'll love it.

## 4.3 Converters

The XAML engine makes a good job at converting object types when data binding. Remember the above examples where it would convert a *string* to a *double* or even a *Brush*? That conversion system can be extended using converters.

Converters are simply classes you write that inherit from the IValueConverter interface. That interface requires you two write two methods: *Convert* is the "standard" one and *ConvertBack* is used only in two-way data bindings. Once you have a converter, you instantiate it and then reference it from your data binding expressions.

Suppose you have a *double* value that needs to be converted to twice its value when it is displayed. Here's how you would go about it. First, you create a class:

```
namespace Maths: {
  public class TwiceConverter : IValueConverter {
    public object Convert(object value,
      Type targetType, object parameter,
      CultureInfo culture)
    {
      return ((int)value)*2;
    }
    // A ConvertBack empty method would be here
  }
}
```

Then you instantiate that class and use it in a binding expression:

```
<Page xmlns:c="clr-namespace:Maths">
  <Page.Resources>
    <c:TwiceConverter x:Key="twiceConv" />
  </Page.Resources>
  <TextBlock Value="{Binding Speed, Converter={Static\
Resource twiceConv}} />
</Page>
```

We'll see later about resources which are a nice way to share objects at the page or application level, for now just take it as a way to instantiate our converter class.

Suppose you have a *double* value that needs to be converted to a color: red when above 10, orange between 4 and 10, and green below 4. Easy, just write your converter. In fact, each time you're going to wonder "how can I achieve that using data binding?", the answer will be: *a converter*. Well, *almost* each time.

## 4.4 Displaying collections using list controls

We just saw about data binding one property at a time, but what you often need to do is allow users to see and update collections of data.

I've got more good news for you: that is also easy and simple. In fact, all of the list controls have an *ItemsSource* property, typed as *IEnumerable*[2]. When you assign a collection to that property, the list control displays all of the collection elements. Yes, it's that simple.

Don't take my word for it and let me show you. Remember about the *Car* class we declared earlier? Let's create a collection of cars:

---

[2]That interface is implemented by every collection in .NET: arrays, stacks, lists, ...

**Code-behind**

```
var cars = new List<Car>();
for (int i = 0; i < 10; i++)
{
  cars.Add(new Car() {
    Speed = i * 10
  });
}
this.DataContext = cars;
```

Now, let's declare a *ListBox* control that will display that collection. Hold your breath: I need very few characters in order to get all of the cars displayed:

**XAML**

```
<ListBox ItemsSource="{Binding}" />
```

This is the result:

BusinessLogic.Car
BusinessLogic.Car
BusinessLogic.Car
BusinessLogic.Car
BusinessLogic.Car
BusinessLogic.Car
BusinessLogic.Car
BusinessLogic.Car
BusinessLogic.Car
BusinessLogic.Car

Note that I could assign the *ItemsSource* property using C# code, but that was a nice way to show you how using the *DataContext* can make things more simple: since the collection of cars is assigned to the current *DataContext*, binding the *ItemsSource* property without any path or source just connects it to the cars collection.

Sure, you noticed that the *ListBox* control doesn't display any car information, it just displays a list of class names. Guess what? We're going to learn about changing that right now.

## 4.5 Customizing list controls

In my previous example, the *ListBox* control displays a list of "BusinessLogic.Car" strings. This is due to the fact that WPF doesn't know how to display an instance of my *Car* class so it calls the *ToString* method of each instance. In turn, the *ToString* method falls back to returning the class name since we didn't override it.

The *ListBox* control has a *DisplayMemberPath* property to which I could provide the car property that it should display. But this is too limited: it displays just one property, displays just text, plus that trick won't work with other list controls. We can do way better.

All of the list controls have the following properties that enable you to customize how their items should be displayed:

- *ItemsPanel* states how the elements should be laid out;
- *ItemTemplate* provides a template that should be repeated for each element;
- *ItemContainerStyle* states how the item should behave when selected or when hovered with the mouse (this property is provided only by controls that enable selection);
- *Template* states how the control itself should be rendered (more about that later).

The *ItemTemplate* property should be a *DataTemplate* that will be repeated for each list item. Elements inside the *DataTemplate* can use data binding expressions in order to connect their properties to the underlying item properties. In fact, the *DataContext* of a *DataTemplate* is the item being displayed.

So, here's how I would display the speeds of all cars:

```xml
<ListBox ItemsSource="{Binding}">
  <ListBox.ItemTemplate>
    <DataTemplate>
      <TextBlock Text="{Binding Speed}" />
    </DataTemplate>
  </ListBox.ItemTemplate>
</ListBox>
```

This was a very simple example. Guess what? List controls can display almost anything, not just text. How about getting a full input interface for each car? Easy:

```xml
<ListBox ItemsSource="{Binding}">
  <ListBox.ItemTemplate>
    <DataTemplate>
      <StackPanel>
        <TextBlock Text="Speed" />
        <TextBox Text="{Binding Speed}" />
        <Slider Value="{Binding Speed}"
            Maximum="100" />
        <TextBlock Text="Color" />
        <Border Height="10">
          <Border.Background>
            <SolidColorBrush
              Color="{Binding Color}" />
          </Border.Background>
        </Border>
        <TextBox Text="{Binding Color}" />
      </StackPanel>
    </DataTemplate>
```

```
</ListBox.ItemTemplate>
</ListBox>
```

Here is the result for the two examples above:

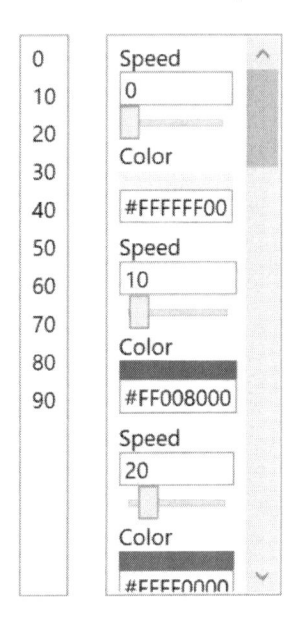

In case you got lost, the following shows a summary of the properties you can use on list controls according to the result you expect:

- **Template** — Around the list (border, background, scrollbars, ...)
- **ItemsPanel** — Items layout
- **ItemTemplate** — Appearance of each item
- **ItemContainerStyle** — Element effects (MouseOver, Selected, ...)

## 4.6 Exercise - Display messages from a data object

Before you begin this exercise, please download some starter files. Follow that link[3] then click the *Download repository* link. That will get you an archive containing the exercises solution and a *StartAssets* folder that we're going to need.

---
[3] https://bitbucket.org/epobb/learnwpfexercises/downloads/

## Managing data in a WPF application

> There is a *Talk.cs* file in the *StartAssets* folder. Add it to your project.
>
> That file defines a *Talk* class which is a collection of messages. Once instantiated it is automatically filled with some sample messages and you can use it right away.
>
> Make sure that the *Discussion.xaml* page you created earlier displays all of the messages contained in the *Talk* instance.
>
> At that point, the *Discussion.xaml* page should look like the following:

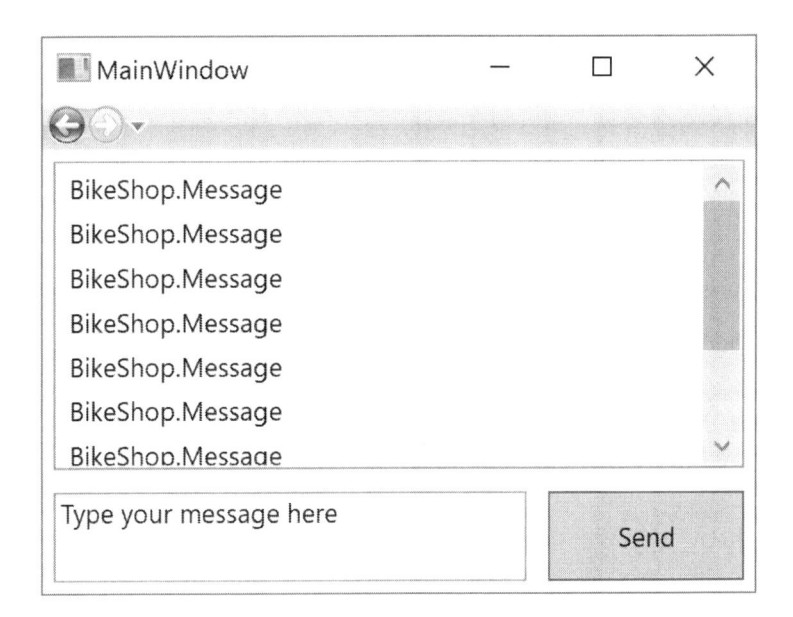

```
MainWindow                        —   □   ×

BikeShop.Message
BikeShop.Message
BikeShop.Message
BikeShop.Message
BikeShop.Message
BikeShop.Message
BikeShop.Message

Type your message here            Send
```

Provide a template to the *ListBox* control so that the page now looks like the following:

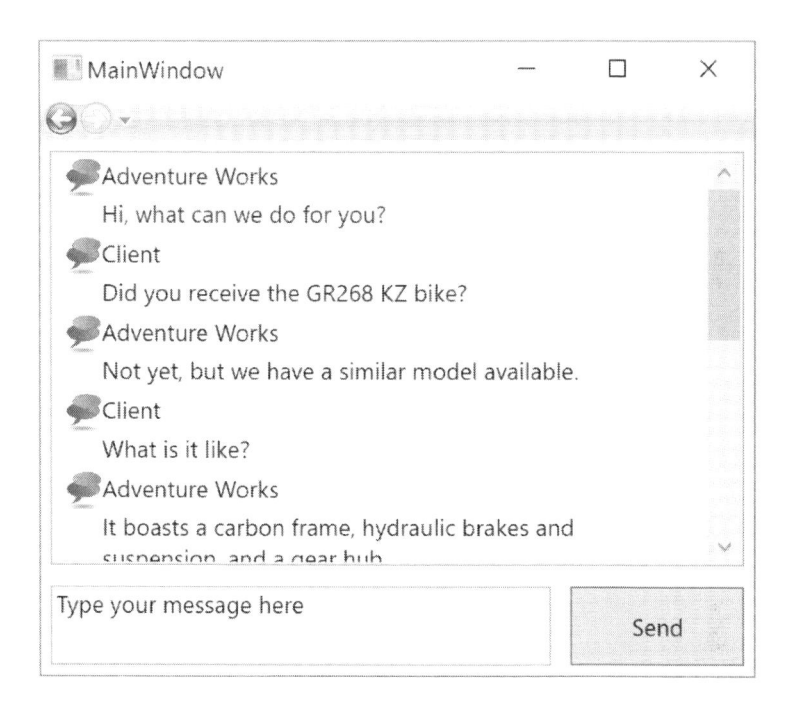

```
MainWindow                                    — □ ×

 Adventure Works
    Hi, what can we do for you?
 Client
    Did you receive the GR268 KZ bike?
 Adventure Works
    Not yet, but we have a similar model available.
 Client
    What is it like?
 Adventure Works
    It boasts a carbon frame, hydraulic brakes and
    suspension, and a gear hub

 Type your message here                    Send
```

## 4.7 Exercise solution

- Switch to Visual Studio.
- Open the *Solution Explorer* clicking on the *View / Solution Explorer* menu entry.
- In the *Solution Explorer*, right-click the project (not the solution), and select *Add / Existing Item…* from

the context menu.
- In the *Add Existing Item* dialog box, browse to the *StartAssets* folder and select the *Talk.cs* file. Click the *Add* button.
- In the *Solution Explorer*, right-click the project (not the solution), and select *Add / Existing Item...* from the context menu.
- In the *Add Existing Item* dialog box, browse to the *StartAssets* folder, change the file type to *All Files* and select the *chat.png* file. Click the *Add* button.
- In the *Solution Explorer*, double-click the *Discussion.xaml* file.
- Locate the *Page* element in the XAML and add the following attribute:

```
xmlns:data="clr-namespace:BikeShop"
```

- Locate the *ListBox* element declaration. Replace it with the following one:

```
<ListBox Grid.ColumnSpan="2"
         Margin="5">
  <ListBox.ItemsSource>
      <data:Talk />
  </ListBox.ItemsSource>
</ListBox>
```

- Run the application (click on the *Debug / Start Debugging* menu entry).

- Click on the "Live support" button. Check that the *Discussion* page displays a list of unformatted entries.
- Close the application.
- Replace the *ListBox* declaration you just wrote with the following one, that includes an *ItemTemplate* property:

```xml
<ListBox Grid.ColumnSpan="2"
         Margin="5">
  <ListBox.ItemsSource>
    <data:Talk />
  </ListBox.ItemsSource>
  <ListBox.ItemTemplate>
    <DataTemplate>
      <StackPanel Width="300">
        <StackPanel Orientation="Horizontal">
          <Image Source="chat.png"
                 Width="20" />
          <TextBlock Text="{Binding Sender}" />
        </StackPanel>
        <TextBlock Text="{Binding Content}"
                   Margin="20,0,0,0"
                   TextWrapping="Wrap" />
      </StackPanel>
    </DataTemplate>
  </ListBox.ItemTemplate>
</ListBox>
```

- Run the application again and check that the list now looks as expected.

- Close the application.

## 4.8 INotifyPropertyChanged

All would be nice in the data binding world if the WPF engine could read our mind. Unfortunately it doesn't. Hence there are use cases that require some more work.

When a property is updated by a user through a control, any other control that is bound to the same property will update without you having any code to write at all. But when a property changes due to the code itself (e.g. in response to an event, or data coming from a web service), the controls bound to it will not update.

For this kind of scenario to work, the property needs to raise an event stating that it changed. And there are good news: it's easy to do, plus most generated classes (Entity Framework, web service and WCF client proxies) raise that event. This event is described in the *INotifyPropertyChanged* interface, which means that practically your data objects should implement the *INotifyPropertyChanged* interface.

Since all of your data objects are going to need it, I recommend you add the following class to all of your projects and inherit your data objects from it:

```csharp
using System.ComponentModel;

public class Notifier : INotifyPropertyChanged
{
  public event PropertyChangedEventHandler
    PropertyChanged;

  protected void OnPropertyChanged(
    string propertyName)
  {
    if(PropertyChanged!=null)
    {
      PropertyChanged(this,
          new PropertyChangedEventArgs(propertyName));
    }
  }
}
```

It's not as complicated as it looks. Most of the code comes easily as you implement the *INotifyPropertyChanged* class. Anyway, if you don't understand it yet you can still use it.

> Most MVVM frameworks provide such a class and even helpers for you to raise that event in some smart ways. But for now I didn't tell you about the MVVM pattern.

Now, when you write a data object class, inherit from your

*Notifier* class and make sure that you call the *OnPropertyChanged* method in your properties' setters.

Remember our car class? It was written like that:

```
public class Car
{
  public double Speed { get; set; }
  public Color Color { get; set; }
  public Human Driver { get; set; }
}
```

In order for the interface to update when the *Speed* property gets updated by code, we should rewrite it as such:

```
public class Car : Notifier
{
  private double speed;

  public double Speed
  {
    get { return speed; }
    set
    {
      speed = value;
      OnPropertyChanged("Speed");
    }
  }

  // Other Car properties
}
```

## 4.9 INotifyCollectionChanged

We just saw about the *INotifyPropertyChanged* interface that enables data objects to notify WPF controls of their properties' changes. Thanks to them you can write clean code that focuses on updating the data objects, while the data-bound UI is updated automatically.

Now, you can go a step further. When a collection's contents change, you can produce fine-grained notification. Going back to the application you created during the exercises, if we used only the *INotifyPropertyChanged* interface, when the user sends or receives a message all the list's contents would need to be removed and added again. A loss of time, especially if the added message is at the end and not even visible due to the current scroll of the *ListBox* control. We can do way better using a more appropriate interface: *INotifyCollectionChanged*.

The *INotifyCollectionChanged* interface allows collections to notify of additions, removals and changes. WPF list controls detect that interface and take it into account in order to update the user interface in a fine-grained way.

And there are good news: you don't even need to implement that interface yourself: WPF comes with a class that is just like *List<T>* except that it implements the *INotifyCollectionChanged* interface: *ObservableCollection<T>*.

Practically, all you need to do is use *ObservableCollection<T>* in lieu of *List<T>* and you get fine-grained UI updates.

## 4.10 Exercise - Display products and details

There are *Notifier.cs* and *ProductsFactory.cs* files in the *StartAssets* folder. Add them to your project.

The *Notifier.cs* contains property change notification code we saw in the INotifyPropertyChanged chapter.

The *ProductsFactory.cs* file defines a *Product* class and a *ProductsFactory* class. The *ProductsFactory* exposes methods that return a list of random products, filtered or not. Have a look at them.

You should create a *ProductsManagement.xaml* page that lists all of the products and looks like the following:

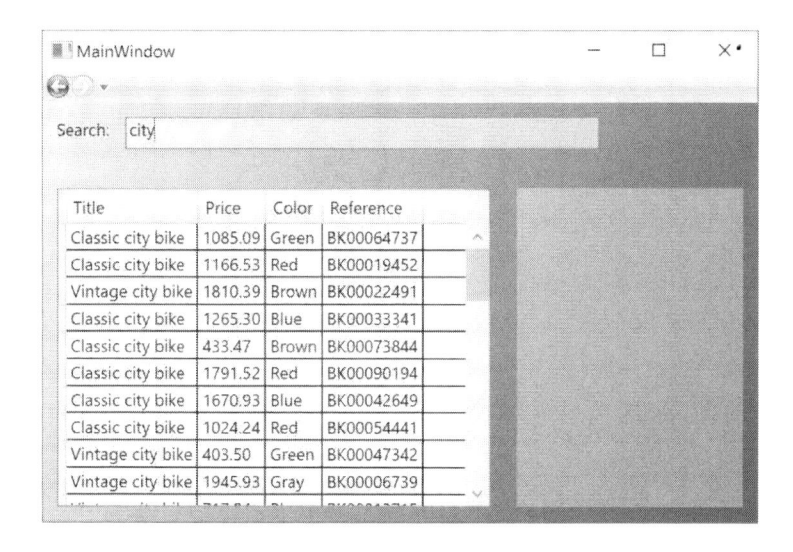

> Make sure that the user navigates to the *ProductsManagement* page when the *Products* button of the *Menu* page is clicked.
>
> When a search string is entered into the *TextBox*, the list should be filtered using it.
>
> When the user selects a product, the product details should be displayed on the right-hand side, as such:

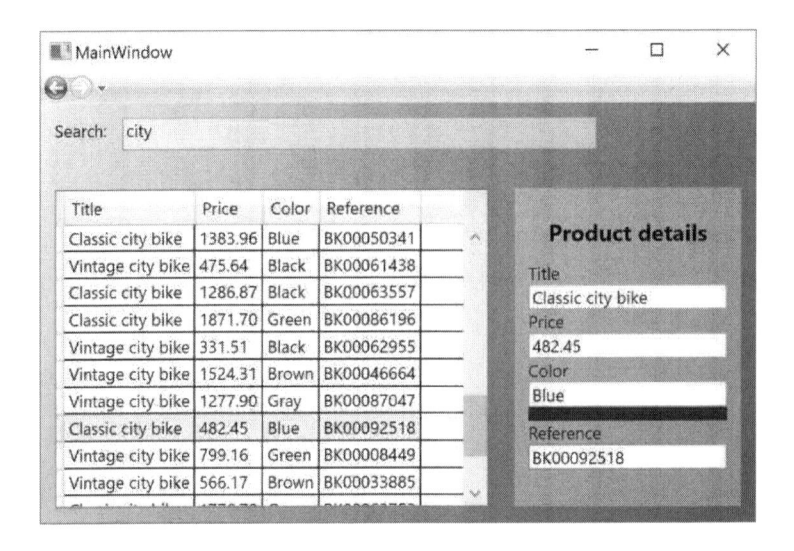

## 4.11 Exercise solution

- Switch to Visual Studio.
- Open the *Solution Explorer* clicking on the *View / Solution Explorer* menu entry.
- In the *Solution Explorer*, right-click the project (not the solution), and select *Add / Existing Item...* from the context menu.
- In the *Add Existing Item* dialog box, browse to the *StartAssets* folder and select the *Notifier.cs* and *ProductsFactory.cs* files. Click the *Add* button.
- In the *Solution Explorer*, right-click the project (not the solution), and select *Add / Page* from the context menu.

- In the *Add New Item* dialog box, look for the *Name* zone at the bottom, and type "ProductsManagement". Click the *Add* button.
- In the *Solution Explorer*, double-click the *ProductsManagement.xaml* file.
- From the *Toolbox* window, add the following controls to the page: a *TextBox* at the top, a *DataGrid* in the center and a *Border* to the right-hand side.
- Assign the following properties to the controls:

| Control | Property | Value |
| --- | --- | --- |
| TextBox | Text | (empty) |
| TextBox | Background | white |
| DataGrid | Name | "dataGrid" |
| Border | Background | white |

- Double-click the *TextBox* control. That creates a *textBox_TextChanged* method.
- Add the following field to the *ProductsManagement* class:

```
ProductsFactory factory = new ProductsFactory();
```

- Add the following code to the *textBox_TextChanged* method:

## 98 Managing data in a WPF application

```
dataGrid.ItemsSource =
  factory.FindProducts(textBox.Text);
```

- Open the *Menu.xaml* file.
- Double-click the button that reads "Products". This adds a *Click* attribute to the XAML, an event handler to the code-behind, and opens the code-behind.
- Add the following code to the created event handler:

```
private void button2_Click(object sender,
  RoutedEventArgs e)
{
    NavigationService.Navigate(
      new Uri(
        "/ProductsManagement.xaml",
        UriKind.Relative
      )
    );
}
```

- Run the application (click on the *Debug / Start Debugging* menu entry).
- Click on the "Products" button. Check that when you type a search string in the *TextBox* control a list of matching products is displayed.
- Close the application.
- Open the *ProductsManagement.xaml* file.
- Add the following *DataContext* attribute to the *Border* element:

```
<Border DataContext="{Binding SelectedItem, ElementNa\
me=dataGrid}"
   ... />
```

- Add the following code inside the *Border* element:

```
<StackPanel Margin="10">
  <TextBlock Text="Product details"
    FontWeight="Bold"
    FontSize="16"
    HorizontalAlignment="Center"
    Margin="10" />
  <TextBlock Text="Title" />
  <TextBox Text="{Binding Title, Mode=TwoWay}" />
  <TextBlock Text="Price" />
  <TextBox Text="{Binding Price, Mode=TwoWay}" />
  <TextBlock Text="Color" />
  <TextBox Text="{Binding Color, Mode=TwoWay}" />
  <Border Background="{Binding Color}"
    Height="10" />
  <TextBlock Text="Reference" />
  <TextBox Text="{Binding Reference, Mode=TwoWay}" />
</StackPanel>
```

- Run the application (click on the *Debug / Start Debugging* menu entry).
- Click on the "Products" button. Type a search string. Check that when you select an product from the *DataGrid* control all of its properties are displayed on the right-hand side panel.

- Change some product properties using the right-hand side panel. Check that the changes are displayed in the *DataGrid* control.
- Close the application.

## I need you, super-hero !

Thank you so much for reading this book. I do hope that it helps you understand and get confident with WPF and MVVM.

As a reader, you are kind of a super-hero: you gain the power to create beautiful and well architectured desktop applications using WPF and make computers more useful.

Guess what? You have another superpower: to rate this book on the site where you purchased it, or Amazon. You may feel it's nothing, but it is super important for auto-edited books like this one. Please, take some minutes of your precious time to rate this book. That counts a lot for independent authors like myself!

# 5. Making it shine: customize the look

## 5.1 Change a control's look

As we saw earlier, WPF controls come with a default appearance that can be changed at will. You'll be surprised how easy it is, and this is just what templating is about.

### Template

Almost every WPF control has a *Template* property. Assign a new *ControlTemplate* instance to this property in order to provide the control with a new appearance. Here is a simple example:

```
<Button Content="Press me">
  <Button.Template>
    <ControlTemplate TargetType="{x:Type Button}">
      <Ellipse Fill="GreenYellow"
        Width="100" Height="100" />
    </ControlTemplate>
  </Button.Template>
</Button>
```

And here's the result:

A very basic and almost awful look, but the *Button* control remains fully functional, raising *Click* or *MouseOver* events as the user interacts with it. Even better: the surface that raises those events isn't rectangular anymore; clicking anywhere outside the disk, even very close to it, won't raise the *Click* event. That's one side thing to learn about templates: any zone that has no content is not part of the control and won't intercept the mouse pointer.

If you look again at the XAML code I just provided for templating, you'll see that in fact there is much boilerplate; apart from that boilerplate it's simple. In fact, there are only a few things to note:

- the new appearance for this control is an *Ellipse*;
- there is a *TargetType* property on the *ControlTemplate* instance.

The *TargetType* property may seem useless since we can obviously see that this *ControlTemplate* applies to a *Button* control, but it's necessary. In fact, you'll very soon find yourself defining templates that are common to several controls (DRY[1] again) storing them as resources, which means they will be defined without any contextual information about the target controls; that's why stating the target type is necessary.

Now, our template is too simple. If you look at the result again, you'll notice that the button content (a "Press me" text) isn't displayed. In fact, if you use that same code you'll notice that the *Button* control doesn't comply with what you state as a developer: resizing it has no effect, neither does assigning a new background color or using other properties of the *Button*. In other words: we just broke that button, at least its compliance. We need something more, and that's what *TemplateBinding* is for.

> Templates are very powerful and you can give almost any look to your controls including animations. However, doing so writing XAML manually is tedious. If you want to get great results, learn to use *Blend for Visual Studio* which is included with Visual Studio. Blend enables you to actually *draw* the control look you want and animate it; it generates the corresponding XAML for you.

---

[1] Don't Repeat Yourself

## TemplateBinding

What we need is, from inside the *ControlTemplate* definition, an ability to refer to the templated control's properties. That way, we could make our template use them. That's exactly what the *TemplateBinding* syntax is for.

Let's improve our previous sample using that syntax:

```
<Button Content="Press me">
  <Button.Template>
    <ControlTemplate TargetType="{x:Type Button}">
      <Grid>
        <Ellipse Fill="{TemplateBinding Background}"
          Width="100"
          Height="100" />
        <Label Content="{TemplateBinding Content}"
          HorizontalAlignment="Center"
          VerticalAlignment="Center" />
      </Grid>
    </ControlTemplate>
  </Button.Template>
</Button>
```

That new appearance displays the button's original content and respects its background:

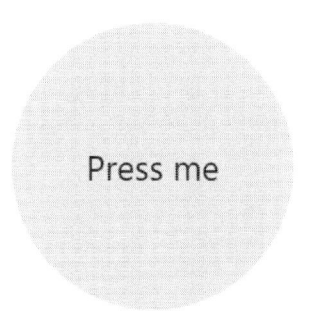

Now, if I assign a background (whatever one: solid, gradient or even a *VisualBrush*) to the control itself, the *Ellipse* control will use it. Great! In the previous screenshot our *Ellipse* is gray because this is the default value of the *Background* property of the *Button* control.

> In the example code above I used a *Label* control in order to render the original content of the *Button*. If I had used a *TextBlock* control I would have been limited to text contents, while a *Label* control allows for any content. Which means anyone who uses our template can assign a *MediaElement*, or even a *ListBox* or a *Grid* with children as the button content, and it will get displayed over the *Ellipse*.

## ItemsPresenter

List controls that have an *Items* property like *ListBox* and *ComboBox* can also be templated. Note that if you want to change the individual look of each element you should use an ItemTemplate. If you want, however, to change the global layout of the control, for instance rotate or scale the items list or create a different kind of shape, you can also use the *Template* property of these controls in order to provide a new appearance.

When creating the template for a list control, you'll find yourself at a point where you want to display the actual list of items (using the *ItemTemplate* and *ItemsPanel* provided, if any). This is where you go for the *ItemsPresenter*. The *ItemsPresenter* control simply needs to be inserted where you want to display the actual items inside the template, and it will do the work for you. No configuration needed. Yes, it's that simple.

## 5.2 Exercise - Create a basic button template

We want to change the appearance of the *Send* button on the *Discussion.xaml* page. Choose a look you like and make sure the original text (*Send*) is displayed. It could be something along those lines:

## 5.3 Exercise solution

- Switch to Visual Studio.
- Open the *Solution Explorer* clicking on the *View / Solution Explorer* menu entry.
- In the *Solution Explorer*, double-click the *Discussion.xaml* file.
- Locate the *Button* element declaration. Add the following code inside the *Button* element:

```
<Button.Template>
  <ControlTemplate TargetType="Button">
    <Grid>
      <Ellipse Fill="#AA000000"
        Margin="10, 10, 0, 0" />
      <Ellipse Fill="{TemplateBinding Background}"
        Margin="0, 0, 10, 10" />
      <Viewbox Margin="5, 5, 15, 15">
        <ContentPresenter />
      </Viewbox>
    </Grid>
  </ControlTemplate>
</Button.Template>
```

- Run the application (click on the *Debug / Start Debugging* menu entry).
- Click on the "Live support" button. Check that the *Discussion* page sports a customized button.
- Close the application.

## 5.4 Resources

Once you write a great template for a control, chances are that you'll want it used in several places across your application. It wouldn't be practical nor maintainable to duplicate the template code. That's where resources shine.

In fact, resources are going to be the answer whenever you need to share some XAML across several controls, whether on the same screen or different screens across your application.

Every control inside the application can store resources using its *Resources* property, which is a string-keyed dictionary. That means you can add any resource object providing it a string key.

The control itself and all of its subcontrols can access the control's resources. Which means that there are mainly two places where we store resources:

- The screen: *Page*, *UserControl* or *Window*, for resources that are scoped to a single screen;
- The application: the *Application* element declared in *App.xaml*, for resources that are used all across the application.

> In fact there's a third place: resource dictionaries. More about that a little later.

That's it for the theory. Let's see how that plays out. Here, we define two resources in the *App.xaml* file:

```
<Application ...>
 <Application.Resources>
  <Button x:Key="button">Hello, world</Button>
  <SolidColorBrush x:Key="accentBrush" Color="Red" />
 </Application.Resources>
</Application>
```

Note how the *Button* and *SolidColorBrush* classes are instantiated in the code above: exactly as they would in any other place, except that we assign a *x:Key* to them. The key is a name we will reuse when referencing those resources. Here's how:

```
<Label Content="{StaticResource button}"
 Background="{StaticResource accentBrush}" />
```

The code above could be placed anywhere in the application since the resources were declared under the *Application* element. Had we wished to scope those resources to a smaller portion of the application, we could have declared them under a *Page* element or a *ResourceDictionary* referenced by a few pages.

The *StaticResource* syntax is simply followed by the key of the resource you want to use: the exact same string as the one assigned using the *x:Key* attribute.

When using resources, the result is the same as if the resources had been declared directly as property values. You should use resources anytime you need to share an object instantiated in XAML.

> If you think about it, a resource declared under the *Application* element is a singleton. Yes, declaring a singleton is easier in XAML than in C#.

One more thing to know about resources: when referencing them you can use a *DynamicResource* syntax instead of the *StaticResource* syntax.

In short: I recommend using the *StaticResource* and there's not much difference.

*DynamicResource* simply has the advantage that if the resource is replaced with another one while being used (e.g. screen still displayed), the result will be immediately visible. This is a scarce use case (especially since resources can implement *INotifyPropertyChanged*) so why bother with the associated overhead?

## ResourceDictionaries

In a real world application you are likely to declare a bunch of resources under the *Application* element: converters, brushes, data objects or technical objects, control templates, data templates. Which means that your *App.xaml* file is likely to grow unmaintainable. Being an organized developer, you surely want to get things organized, and that's what resource dictionaries are made for.

Using resource dictionaries is easy: just add some "resource dictionary" files to your project, and place your resources inside them (they are plain XAML files). Then, reference them from any *Resources* property adding the following kind of declaration:

```
<Window.Resources>
  <ResourceDictionary Source="Brushes.xaml" />
</Window.Resources>
```

## 5.5 Exercise - Set the background

Make sure that all of the pages you created share a common background (choose some colors you like). That background should be stored as a resource in order for it to be shared.

Note that depending on the version of WPF and Visual Studio, using implicit styles for pages may not work in the design view or at run time. Plus I didn't teach you about styles yet. So please don't use styles for that exercise.

## 5.6 Exercise solution

- Switch to Visual Studio.

- Open the *Solution Explorer* clicking on the *View / Solution Explorer* menu entry.
- In the *Solution Explorer*, double-click the *App.xaml* file.
- Under the *Application.Resources* element add the following XAML code:

```
<LinearGradientBrush x:Key="background">
  <GradientStop Color="#FFDBFFE7"
    Offset="0" />
  <GradientStop Color="#FF03882D"
    Offset="1" />
</LinearGradientBrush>
```

- Open the *Contact.xaml*, *Discussion.xaml*, *Menu.xaml* and *ProductsManagement.xaml* pages. For each of them, add the following *Background* attribute to the *Page* element:

```
<Page ...
  Background="{StaticResource background}">
```

- Run the application (click on the *Debug / Start Debugging* menu entry).
- Check that all of the pages show a gradient background.
- Close the application.

## 5.7 Styles

Styles, as their name suggests, are a good way to style the appearance of controls. But we already saw a bunch of ways to style controls: templates, properties and resources. So why bother with styles?

In order to understand styles, you should think of them as "multi property setters", which is what they are. Suppose you need to set the background of several *Button* controls to some nice gradient brush: you could get away with a resource and that would be fine. But suppose you need to set the background to some gradient brush *and* the height and width to some standard value. Then you would need to define three resources and reference them from each *Button* control's three properties: *Background*, *Width* and *Height*. Styles allow you to do just that, in a concise way.

Here is the declaration I could use for the style I just mentioned:

```
<Application.Resources>
  <Style x:Key="niceButton"
      TargetType="Button">
    <Setter Property="Width"
      Value="50" />
    <Setter Property="Height"
      Value="50" />
    <Setter Property="Background">
      <Setter.Value>
        <LinearGradientBrush>
```

```xml
            <GradientStop Color="Red" />
            <GradientStop Color="Yellow" Offset="1" />
        </LinearGradientBrush>
      </Setter.Value>
    </Setter>
  </Style>
</Application.Resources>
```

And here is how I would apply my style to some buttons:

```xml
<StackPanel Margin="50">
  <Button Style="{StaticResource niceButton}">
    A
  </Button>
  <Button>
    B
  </Button>
  <Button Style="{StaticResource niceButton}">
    C
  </Button>
  <Button Style="{StaticResource niceButton}">
    D
  </Button>
</StackPanel>
```

This is the result:

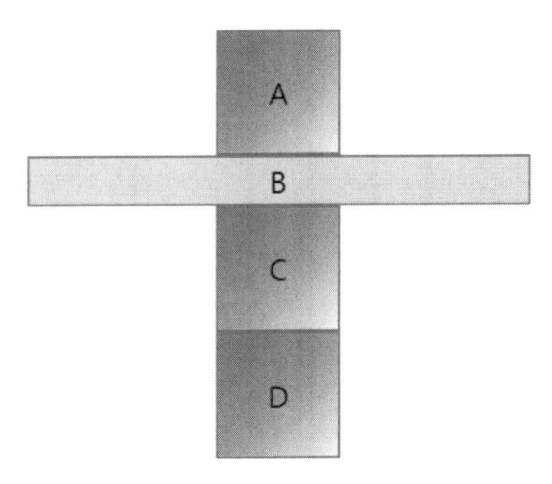

The second button is not styled since we didn't explicitly assign a style.

Now, there's one more thing: implicit styles. Styles (and templates) can be stored as resources without assigning a key to them. In that case, they will be automatically used for all of the controls matching their *TargetType* within their scope. For instance, the following XAML would style all of the controls on the page:

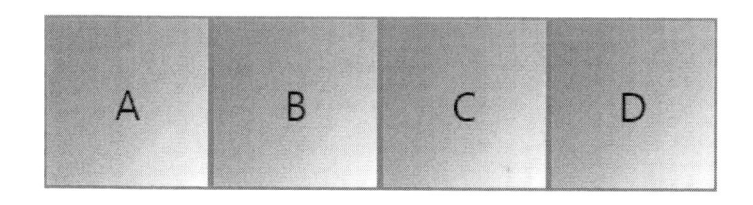

```xml
<Page ...>
  <Page.Resources>
    <Style TargetType="Button">
      ...
    </Style>
  </Page.Resources>
  <StackPanel Orientation="Horizontal">
    <Button>A</Button>
    <Button>B</Button>
    <Button>C</Button>
    <Button>D</Button>
  </StackPanel>
</Page>
```

Implicit styles are a great way to provide styling for controls of a whole application. For finer grained styling, simply use keyed styles.

## 5.8 Exercise - Improve menu page using an implicit style

We want to change the appearance of every *Send* button on the *Menu.xaml* page. Use the template you created in the previous exercise. Your menu page should look like:

## 5.9 Exercise solution

- Switch to Visual Studio.
- Open the *Solution Explorer* clicking on the *View / Solution Explorer* menu entry.

- In the *Solution Explorer*, double-click the *Menu.xaml* file.
- Add the following code right under to the root page element:

```
<Page.Resources>
  <Style TargetType="Button">
    <Setter Property="Template">
      <Setter.Value>
        <ControlTemplate />
      </Setter.Value>
    </Setter>
  </Style>
</Page.Resources>
```

- Replace the `<ControlTemplate />` element with the *ControlTemplate* you declared in the previous exercise.
- Run the application (click on the *Debug / Start Debugging* menu entry).
- Check the the menu page uses your new templated button for its three buttons.
- Close the application.

## 5.10 Themes

If you work with a designer correctly, she'll probably provide you with some *ResourceDictionary* files containing implicitly and explicitly styles that apply templates and property values. That could be called a *theme*.

You probably wonder if there are any freely available themes in case you don't work with a designer, like it would be the case for small projects. Well, yes. You can find several themes here[2] for instance.

## 5.11 Transforms

It's easy to scale, rotate, or even skew any control. All controls have a *RenderTransform* and *LayoutTransform* available for this. Both accept the exact same children that describe the transformation to apply; their difference is how they take it into account for computing the required size.

You could write the XAML needed for transformations yourself but it's pointless: Visual Studio allows you to do so in an intuitive way. Just open the *Properties* window for a control and you'll find a *Transform* section that looks like that:

---

[2] https://wpfthemes.codeplex.com

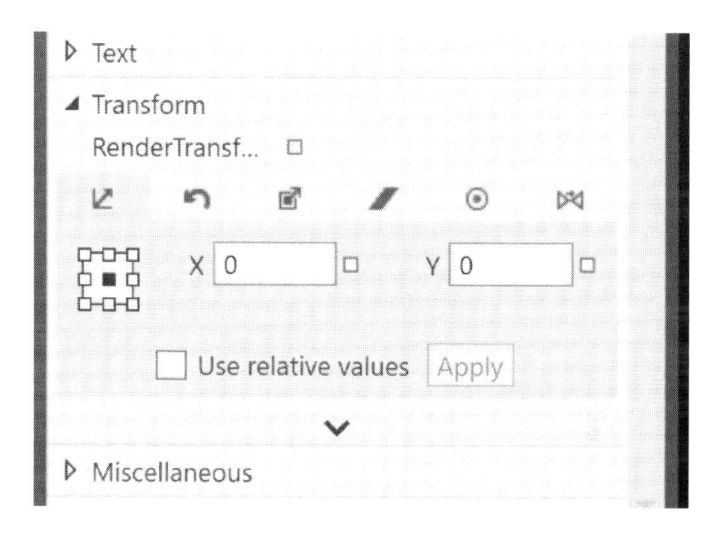

If you watch closely you'll see that there is an expander at the bottom that enables you to access the less used *LayoutTransform*. So what's the difference? Easy: *RenderTransform* doesn't take into account the transformation when computing the needed size for your control (see Size allocation if needed), while *LayoutTransform* does. When working in design mode or over a *Canvas* there's no difference, that's why *LayoutTransform* isn't used very much.

In case that wasn't clear, here's the difference between both:

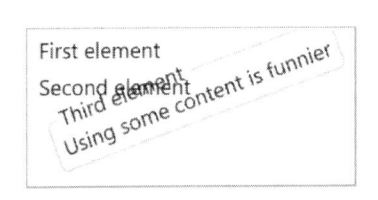

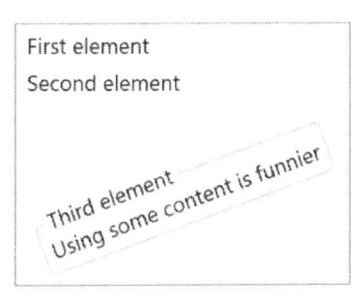

On the left, I used a *RenderTransform* so the size allocated to the *GroupBox* control inside the *ListBox* is the one it would have had if it hadn't been transformed. That's why it overwrites the other elements once rotated.

## 5.12 Control states

If you tried creating a template for a *Button* control using the tools we saw, you may be disappointed: its appearance doesn't change when clicked, nor does it when the mouse enters its zone. We can do better. Sure, you immediately think about animations and we'll talk about animations shortly, but this is not what I recommend.

If you try animations, you'll need to make one for the mouse being pressed, another one for the mouse being released, plus one for the mouse entering and one for the mouse exiting the control zone. Oh, and one for the mouse entering the zone and being pressed at the same time, and the reverse one. That makes six animations, which are interdependent. Think of the hell you prepare yourself should you go that way.

There's a better way: control states. They allow you to think in terms of the appearance your control has in each state, and WPF will animate any transition between the states. In the case of a button, instead of six animations you end up modifying the appearance in two states (*Pressed* and *MouseOver*). That's much, much less work.

Some theory first: each control declares their own list of states using attributes. Here's an extract from the *Button* declaration:

```
[TemplateVisualState(Name = "Normal",
  GroupName = "CommonStates")]
[TemplateVisualState(Name = "MouseOver",
  GroupName = "CommonStates")]
[TemplateVisualState(Name = "Pressed",
  GroupName = "CommonStates")]
[TemplateVisualState(Name = "Disabled",
  GroupName = "CommonStates")]
[TemplateVisualState(Name = "Unfocused",
  GroupName = "FocusStates")]
[TemplateVisualState(Name = "Focused",
  GroupName = "FocusStates")]
public class Button : ButtonBase { ... }
```

As you can see, states can be grouped. They are mutually exclusive inside a group but a control can be at the same time in several states from different groups. In your screen, some XAML code is added that describes the expected changes when transitioning to a state. *Blend for Visual Studio* will generate it for you with a few mouse operations, but here's how it could look like:

```
<ControlTemplate
  TargetType="Button"
  xmlns:vsm="clr-namespace:System.Windows;assembly=Sy\
stem.Windows">
<Border x:Name="RootElement">
  <vsm:VisualStateManager.VisualStateGroups>
    <vsm:VisualStateGroup x:Name="CommonStates">
      <vsm:VisualState x:Name="MouseOver">
        <Storyboard>
          <ColorAnimation
            Storyboard.TargetName="BorderBrush"
            Storyboard.TargetProperty="Color"
            To="Red" />
        </Storyboard>
      </vsm:VisualState>
...
```

Then, the transitions can be animated by simply specifying something like:

```
<vsm:VisualTransition GeneratedDuration="0:0:1.5">
```

For further controls, you can even use the *From* and *To* properties of a *VisualTransition* in order to have a different timing on specific state transitions, like a shorter one when entering the *Pressed* state of a *Button* control.

As I wrote, *Blend for Visual Studio* will generate the XAML for you. What you need to do is:

- enter the *Template* definition mode (right-click the control and select *Template / Edit Current*);

- open the *States* window;
- click on the state name you wish to edit;
- make the required changes by changing control properties or moving them around;
- optionally, specify a transition duration clicking on the group name in the *States* window.

> States are not limited to control templates. In any screen you can declare your own list of states and switch between them using XAML or C#. And you get the same handy animated transitions.

## 5.13 Animations

States are an easy way to create animations in most situations. They allow for easy maintenance of the animations since they focus on final states, not transition details.

You may however want to sometimes customize the way transitions are made, for instance split them in several different steps. In that case, you can create a custom animation using a *StoryBoard*.

A *StoryBoard* is also the perfect candidate when you want to do one-way animations, for instance have a sun rise over your application during the course of the day and have the general background color change accordingly.

An animation is declared using XAML and stored as a resource. Here is a sample animation:

```
<Page.Resources>
 <Storyboard x:Key="rotateFast">
  <DoubleAnimationUsingKeyFrames
    BeginTime="00:00:00"
    Storyboard.TargetName="rotation"
    Storyboard.TargetProperty="Angle">
   <SplineDoubleKeyFrame KeyTime="00:00:02"
    Value="90"/>
  </DoubleAnimationUsingKeyFrames>
 </Storyboard>
</Page.Resources>
```

Once an animation has been declared, it can be triggered using XAML code (triggers) or C#. Here is what we can write in the code-behind for that page in order to get the *rotateFast* animation started:

```
rotateFast.Begin();
```

Mind you: animation code can be tedious. If you are going to create animations, I recommend using *Blend for Visual Studio* since it allows for an easy timeline-view edition of the animation. *Blend for Visual Studio* also allows you to preview an animation and check its appearance at any point in time. In short: use *Blend for Visual Studio* when creating animations.

In Blend, you simply click the "+" button at the top of the *Objects and Timeline* window in order to create a *StoryBoard*. As a result, the storyboard editor is shown:

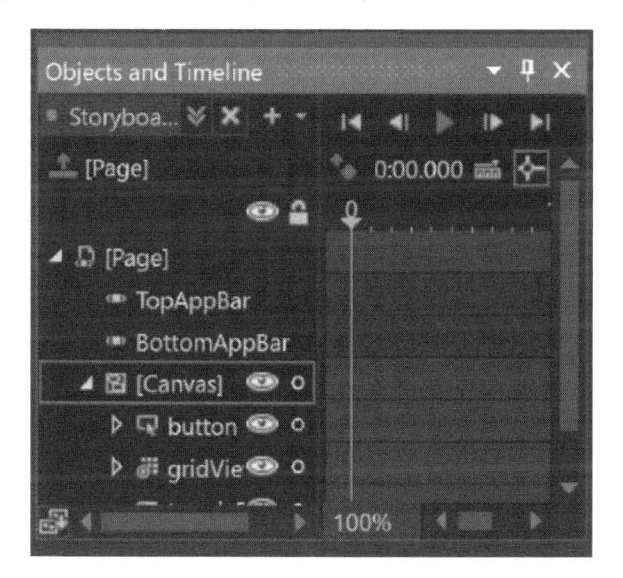

You then move the yellow vertical line along the timeline, and change object properties. Those changes are recorded as XAML in the *StoryBoard*, and Blend shows them with a gray marker that appears at the crossroad of the yellow line and object name:

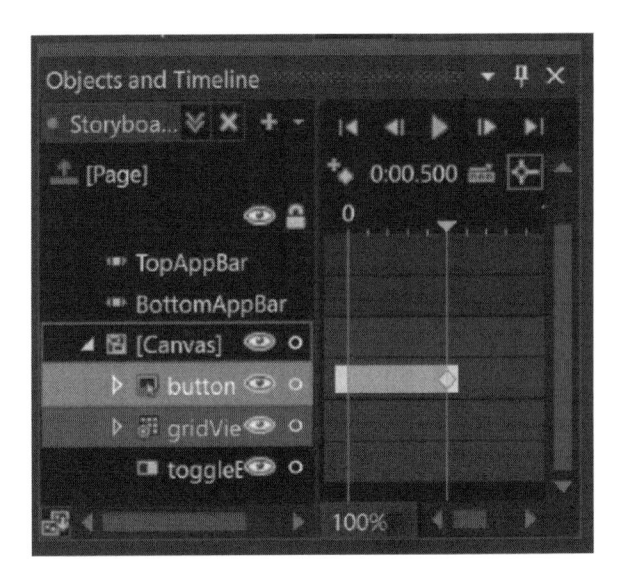

That's really all there is to it! I've seen some developers declare *StoryBoard* objects using C# because they didn't know about Blend or didn't dare to learn using it, and man they had a really hard, hard time.

# 6. MVVM pattern for WPF

## 6.1 Spaghetti code

If you take no care, you can end up writing unmaintainable, non reusable code. It can happen really fast, in fact. Here is an example fictitious code that could be the code-behind for a WPF or Windows Forms screen:

```
void Loaded(object sender,
   RoutedEventArgs args)
{
   BankData = GetBankData();
   BankData.DataChanged +=
      new EventHandler(BankData_Changed);
}

void BankData_Changed(
   object sender,
   BankDataEventArgs args)
{
   BankData b = args.Data;
   this.BalanceDisplay = b.Balance;
   if(this.IncludeInterests.Checked)
   {
      this.BalanceDisplay =
         b.Balance * b.InterestRate;
```

129

    }
}

```
void BalanceDisplay_TextChanged(
  object sender,
  RoutedEventArgs args)
{
    ...
}
```

There are many problems with that kind of code:

- It makes huge files, which in turn make it more difficult to maintain. That kind of code often produces more than 5000 lines of code-behind for one screen.
- It's difficult to test: since the controls' code and logical code are deeply mixed, the UI needs to be instantiated in order for tests to be ran.
- It's hardly reusable: reference to the controls make it tedious to reuse the code on another screen.
- It's deeply aware of the controls' properties: any change to the UI will have a high impact on that code.

I could go on and on with that list. In short, that way of coding produces unmaintainable code.

However, it's a code that is natural to write, hence many applications are coded in that way. That's *spaghetti* code, because everything is deeply mixed together. Our concern though should be not to write such code. This is where better patterns like MVC and MVVM come to play. However those patterns bring their own complexity.

## 6.2 MVC

In the past, a better model came out: MVC, which stands for Model View Controller. Basically a controller gets a model and a view, and provides the model to the view. That's fine, and it so happens that WPF has everything for MVC to be coded out of the box:

- View: pure XAML.
- Model: classes implementing *INotifyPropertyChanged* and *INotifyCollectionChanged*.
- Controller: Commands, Triggers, routed events, NavigationService.

But there are two things that created the need for another SOC[1] model:

- just because;
- in order for an architect to know if the developer coded right, she needs to look at your code.

So architects[2] just came in with the MVVM model. MVVM has several advantages, one of which is the fact that an

---
[1] Separation of Concerns
[2] It so happens that I'm also a software architect

architect can tell in one second whether the developer coded right: there should be no code-behind. Easy!

Apart from making architects' code reviews much easier, MVVM brings a clean, reusable, testable (with automated unit testing), maintainable way of coding. Which, in my opinion, are completely worth the extra complexity. I wouldn't recommend MVVM to a developer that works alone on a project and is a beginner to WPF, otherwise it's good practice.

## 6.3 MVVM

MVVM stands for Model View ViewModel. Here's how those parts are related together:

View ▷ ViewModel ▷ DataModel

**DataModel** is made of your business classes. It holds the data provided to the UI. It can be easily unit-tested and good news: you already know how to produce it.

**View** is the UI. Ideally, it's made of pure XAML. It's difficult to test using automated tests, and that's why we want to reduce the amount of code there. As we'll see, the *DataContext* of a view is a *ViewModel*, and data binding serves as the glue between them.

**ViewModel** is the big deal, the thing you need to learn at this point in order to use MVVM. It:

- exposes data as properties and actions as methods (or commands) for one view;
- is very dependent on the view, though it must not reference the view;
- allows for mixing different DataModels, or hide the complexity behind asynchronous calls;
- can be easily unit-tested;
- implements *INotifyPropertyChanged*.

> There are several flavors of MVVM. Over my years of teaching, coding and reviewing WPF code I've come to a method that offers good balance between ease of learning and architectural perfection. It's the one I'll teach you below. Though it can be debated, I believe it serves both as a good learning ground and immediately usable methodology.

## 6.4 Recommended steps (simple)

MVVM can be quite complex especially if you've been kind of spoiled by the code-behind (spaghetti) model associated with Windows Forms or easy WPF. Let's make it as easy as possible: when going with MVVM in order to code a screen, just follow those steps:

1. Create a ViewModel.

2. Find out which properties the ViewModel should expose.
3. Code notifying properties.
4. Use the ViewModel as the DataContext of the View.
5. Databind the View to the ViewModel.
6. Code the functional logic (can be done anytime after step 3).

## Create a ViewModel

The ViewModel simply is a class. There should be one for each screen[3]. With some practice you may want to share a ViewModel across similar screens, or even have base ViewModel classes from which you inherit, but one ViewModel for each screen is a good beginning.

The ViewModel class should implement *INotifyProperty-Changed*. Just inherit it from the *Notifier* class we saw in the INotifyPropertyChanged chapter.

I recommend you name your ViewModel class after the screen. You may have for instance the following files:

- View: \Views\YourScreen.xaml
- ViewModel: \ViewModels\YourScreenViewModel.cs

Or for simple projects:

- View: \Screens\YourScreen.xaml
- ViewModel: \Screens\YourScreenViewModel.cs

[3] A unit of UI: Window, Page or UserControl

## Find out which properties the ViewModel should expose

Just look at the view you want to create (XAML in case you already created it). For any user input or output, you need to add a property to the ViewModel.

## Code notifying properties

The properties you add to the ViewModel should be notifying properties. There are several tools to help simplify that kind of code. If you have no such tool, a notifying property will be coded like that:

```
private double speed;

public double Speed
{
  get { return speed; }
  set
  {
    speed = value;
    OnPropertyChanged("Speed");
  }
}
```

For an explanation about that, read again the INotifyPropertyChanged chapter. The rationale for having notifying properties is that the ViewModel doesn't know about the View, so this is how it can tell "hey, something has changed!"

> Notifying properties take quite some space, but contain no functional code. I suggest you group them in a #region element so they don't take up screen real estate.

At some point, you may want your ViewModel to do something when one of those properties changes. My advice is to add a method in your ViewModel and call it from the property setter with a single line. That way you don't pollute the property declaration with functional code, and when you read a ViewModel you can safely ignore all of the properties' code (which amounts to quite some code in a ViewModel). Last but not least, following .NET naming good practices, that method should be called On[property_name]Changed. The above property would look like:

```
private double speed;

public double Speed
{
  get { return speed; }
  set
  {
    speed = value;
    OnPropertyChanged("Speed");
    OnSpeedChanged();
  }
}
```

```
}

void OnSpeedChanged()
{
  // Add functional code
}
```

## Use the ViewModel as the DataContext of the View

That's the last step. There are many ways to do that. The two easiest ways are using XAML and using code-behind.

### Assign datacontext using XAML

```
<Window xmlns:vm="clr-namespace:ViewModels"
  ...>
  <Window.DataContext>
    <vm:YourScreenViewModel />
  </Window.DataContext>
  ...
</Window>
```

A drawback of this technique is that the ViewModel class gets instantiated when displaying the design view. There are many ways to solve that problem though.

**Assign datacontext using code-behind**

```
public partial class YourScreen: Window
{
  public YourScreen()
  {
    InitializeComponent();
    this.DataContext = new YourScreenViewModel();
  }
}
```

A drawback of this technique is that during design view you get no assistance from the data-binding editor. Read next chapter for a solution.

Note that when using MVVM there should be no code-behind. This is the only code-behind line I'll tolerate if I ever audit your code.

> I'm not that strict. Some special use cases like poorly written controls may require code-behind.

## Use the ViewModel: demanding version

Assigning the DataContext in XAML or code-behind both have drawbacks. There are several solutions depending on the level of complexity you need. A middle ground solution in order to get run-time only ViewModel instantiation **and** data-binding editor is the following one.

Just use a *d:DataContext* attribute in the XAML that specifies your class: that way it doesn't get instantiated during design view but you still get help from the data-binding editor.

```
<Window xmlns:vm="clr-namespace:ViewModels"
  mc:Ignorable="d"
  xmlns:d="http://schemas.microsoft.com/expression/bl\end/2008"
    d:DataContext="{d:DesignInstance vm:YourScreenViewM\odel}"
    ...>
    ...
</Window>
```

Then, assign the DataContext using code-behind, for instance:

```
public partial class YourScreen: Window
{
  public YourScreen()
  {
    InitializeComponent();
    this.DataContext = new YourScreenViewModel();
  }
}
```

## 6.5 Example

At this point I'd like to show you an example. Since we didn't see how to handle actions (commands and methods), it's going to be basic at this point. So let's create a simple currency converter: an amount is input in Euros and I want to know how much it is in US Dollars. Here's what my view looks like:

[CurrencyConverter window with "Amount in €" input field and "Amount in US $ TextBlock"]

Step 1, I create the ViewModel:

```
public class CurrencyConverterViewModel : Notifier
{
}
```

Step 2, let's find out the properties needed. There is one input, the amount in Euros, and one output, the amount in US Dollars. So we need two properties.

Step 3, code the properties. Verbose but very straightforward:

```csharp
private decimal euros;

public decimal Euros
{
  get { return euros; }
  set
  {
    euros = value;
    OnPropertyChanged("Euros");
  }
}

private decimal dollars;

public decimal Dollars
{
  get { return dollars; }
  set
  {
    dollars = value;
    OnPropertyChanged("Dollars");
  }
}
```

Step 4, use the ViewModel as the DataContext of the view. In the XAML (View) I write:

```
<Window xmlns:vm="clr-namespace:MyNameSpace"
 ...>
  <Window.DataContext>
    <vm:CurrencyConverterViewModel />
  </Window.DataContext>
  ...
</Window>
```

Step 5, data-binding. We just need to bind the *Text* properties of the text controls:

```
...
<TextBox Text="{Binding Euros}" ... />
<TextBlock Text="{Binding Dollars}" ... />
...
```

> Note that you even get IntelliSense help for the property names when writing the binding expression. Insanely cool, isn't it?

Step 6, code the functional logic. Back in the ViewModel, I add a call to a *OnEurosChanged* method in the setter of the *Euros* property, then I code that method:

```
private void OnEurosChanged()
{
  Dollars = Euros * 1.1M;
}
```

That's it! We have a fully working screen. That was simple, wasn't it?

## 6.6 Example, more complex

Now let's make things trickier and add a combo box that the user will use in order to select a currency. The screen looks like that:

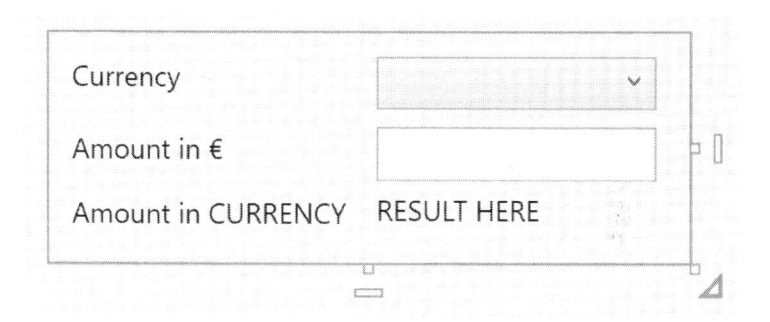

We need the same properties as before, plus three more: one that returns a list of available currencies, one that contains the selected currency, and another for the caption that contains the selected currency. Plus a data object (the Model) class that describes the name and exchange rate of a currency.

Here's the code for the Model and ViewModel. Again, the properties take up most of the space but they contain straightforward code. Ideally the Model properties should notify, but we'll save space here since this use case doesn't require a notifying model.

```
public class Currency
{
  public Currency(string title, decimal rate)
  {
    Title = title;
    Rate = rate;
  }
  public string Title { get; set; }
  public decimal Rate { get; set; }
}

public class CurrencyConverterViewModel2 : Notifier
{
  // Verbose code we can almost ignore
  private decimal euros;

  public decimal Euros
  {
    get { return euros; }
    set
    {
      euros = value;
      OnPropertyChanged("Euros");
      OnEurosChanged();
    }
```

```csharp
}

private decimal converted;

public decimal Converted
{
  get { return converted; }
  set
  {
    converted = value;
    OnPropertyChanged("Converted");
  }
}

private Currency selectedCurrency;

public Currency SelectedCurrency
{
  get { return selectedCurrency; }
  set { selectedCurrency = value;
    OnPropertyChanged("SelectedCurrency");
    OnSelectedCurrencyChanged();
  }
}

private IEnumerable<Currency> currencies;

public IEnumerable<Currency> Currencies
{
  get { return currencies; }
  set { currencies = value;
```

```
    OnPropertyChanged("Currencies");
  }
}

private string resultText;

public string ResultText
{
  get { return resultText; }
  set { resultText = value;
    OnPropertyChanged("ResultText");
  }
}


// This is where the magic happens
public CurrencyConverterViewModel2()
{
  Currencies = new Currency[] {
    new Currency("US Dollar", 1.1M),
    new Currency("British Pound", 0.9M),
  };
}

private void OnEurosChanged()
{
  ComputeConverted();
}
private void OnSelectedCurrencyChanged()
{
  ComputeConverted();
```

```
  }

  private void ComputeConverted()
  {
    if (SelectedCurrency == null)
    {
      return;
    }
    Converted = Euros * SelectedCurrency.Rate;
    ResultText = string.Format(
      "Amount in {0}", SelectedCurrency.Title);
  }
}
```

And now, for the data-bindings in the View:

```
<TextBox Text="{Binding Euros}" ... />
<TextBlock Text="{Binding Converted}" ... />
<TextBlock Text="{Binding ResultText}" ... />
<ComboBox ...
  SelectedItem="{Binding SelectedCurrency}"
  ItemsSource="{Binding Currencies}">
  <ComboBox.ItemTemplate>
    <DataTemplate>
      <TextBlock Text="{Binding Title}" />
    </DataTemplate>
  </ComboBox.ItemTemplate>
</ComboBox>
```

Did you note how the process of creating the ViewModel was straightforward applying the steps I listed? I recommend you stick with those steps for the next months of your MVVM practice, just so they become automatic. Once you do, MVVM will seem simple, even basic.

You may think that we wrote a lot of code for that example, but if you look closer you'll see we didn't. Look again at the ViewModel code: most of it are just property declarations. Though notifying properties are verbose, they are kind of empty and you can just skip them when reading that code. Next, note how the functional logic is concentrated within the *ComputeConverted* method: no reference to controls, just pure functional code. That will make maintenance easy. And this is one of the strengths of MVVM.

Finally, look at how the ViewModel code is separate from the View. It simply doesn't know about the View, so you could add other selectors for the currency, display the typed amount or exchange rate in another *TextBlock* without ever changing the ViewModel. For instance, if I want to display the exchange rate that corresponds to the selected currency all I have to write in he XAML is:

```
<TextBlock Text="{Binding SelectedCurrency.Rate}" ...\
/>
```

## 6.7 Commands and methods

Let's be honest: in my two samples, I was lucky. I could know about user interactions thanks to the *Text* property of the *TextBox* (since she would type text in) and the

*SelectedItem* property of the *ComboBox* control. Often times, we only want to know when the user presses a button. It's not awfully hard to manage but we need to learn one more thing.

## Commands: the apparently easy way

WPF includes an *ICommand* interface. If you implement it with a class and instantiate that class, you can reference that instance using the *Command* property of *Button* and *MenuItem* controls. When those controls are clicked, the command is invoked and that's it.

That would seem like the natural way to go, but it's not. For several reasons.

First, implementing *ICommand* takes quite some code. Hopefully most MVVM frameworks provide you with a *DelegateCommand* class (name varies) that makes that process much less verbose.

Second, you need to assign the instantiated command to a property of your ViewModel. Not awfully difficult, but that means more empty code.

Third - and this is the worse - only the *Click* event triggers the command. End of the show. In order to handle other events like a *MouseOver*, you need to use some verbose XAML which happens to be the same that the one used with methods. This is the kind of code, just for your information:

```
<Button>
  <i:Interaction.Triggers>
    <i:EventTrigger EventName="Click">
      <i:InvokeCommandAction
        Command="{Binding LoadMoreHotelsCommand}"/>
    </i:EventTrigger>
  </i:Interaction.Triggers>
</Button>
```

The natural question is now: why use commands? My answer is: don't. Don't bother with them. Methods will do just fine, so read on.

## Methods: the straightforward way

With methods, the ViewModel C# gets very easy, and the XAML more complex. In fact, just as complex as it would with commands that handle events other than clicks.

> All those considerations about complexity could be mitigated using the right MVVM frameworks or some extensions. My recommendations are based on the barebone toolbox we have using Visual Studio 2015. Also, in case you happen to use *Blend for Visual Studio*, it can generate the XAML for you using a simple drag and drop.

So, using methods is just that: add public methods to your ViewModel. That way, they can be easily accessed using C# (of course), but let's see how we can invoke them in response to control events using XAML.

Once in your project: add a reference to:

```
System.Windows.Interactivity.dll
```

You may do so using NuGet, or you can find it in a folder like:

```
C:\Program Files (x86)\Microsoft SDKs\Expression\Blen\
d\.NETFramework\v4.5\Libraries\
```

Next, in XAML, add the following attributes to the root element of your screen (window, page, user control):

```
xmlns:i="http://schemas.microsoft.com/expression/2010\
/interactivity"
xmlns:ei="http://schemas.microsoft.com/expression/201\
0/interactions"
```

And finally, once for each control and event, you need to add a trigger to the control, in the XAML. It looks like this:

```
<Button>
  <i:Interaction.Triggers>
    <i:EventTrigger EventName="Click">
      <i:CallMethodAction TargetObject="{Binding}"
        Method="LoadMoreHotelsAction"/>
    </i:EventTrigger>
  </i:Interaction.Triggers>
</Button>
```

As I wrote earlier, this code can be generated by *Blend for Visual Studio*: in case you defined your ViewModel as the *DataContext* using XAML, public methods should appear in the "Data context" window and you can simply drag and drop them to the controls. And by the way, this trick also works for normal properties binding.

This XAML code is not that hard anyway. You just state the event name, and method name. It will be invoked on the ViewModel since the *TargetObject* is stated to be the current *DataContext* which is... the ViewModel. Unless you didn't follow my steps.

Easy, right? Well that's it, you know MVVM!

## 6.8 Recommended steps (complete)

Here's the complete list of steps for creating a MVVM screen in a straightforward way:

1. Create a ViewModel.

2. Find out which properties (inputs, outputs) and methods (actions) the ViewModel should expose.
3. Declare notifying properties and add public methods.
4. Use the ViewModel as the DataContext of the View.
5. Databind the View to the ViewModel properties.
6. Add triggers in the View that invoke the ViewModel methods.
7. Code the functional logic (can be done anytime after step 3).

## 6.9 Exercise - Display products and details using MVVM

Add a page named *ProductsManagementMVVM* that behaves exactly as the one you created in the Display products and details exercise. Change the *Menu* code so that this new MVVM version is used instead of the code-behind version when the *Products* button of the menu is clicked.

Just in case, here is a screenshot of the page (again, that's the same as before):

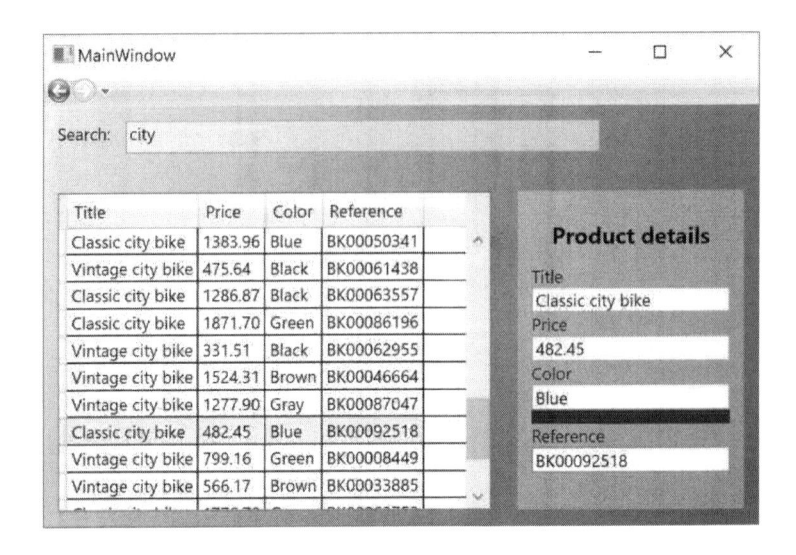

## 6.10 Exercise solution

- Switch to Visual Studio.
- Open the *Solution Explorer* clicking on the *View / Solution Explorer* menu entry.
- In the *Solution Explorer*, right-click the project (not the solution), and select *Add / Page* from the context menu.
- In the *Add New Item* dialog box, look for the *Name* zone at the bottom, and type "ProductsManagementMVVM". Click the *Add* button.
- In the *Solution Explorer*, double-click the *ProductsManagementMVVM.xaml* file.
- From the *Toolbox* window, add the following controls to the page: a *TextBox* at the top, a *DataGrid*

in the center and a *Border* to the right-hand side.
- Assign the following properties to the controls:

| Control | Property | Value |
|---------|----------|-------|
| TextBox | Background | white |
| Border | Background | white |

- In the *Solution Explorer*, right-click the project (not the solution), and select *Add / Class* from the context menu.
- In the *Add New Item* dialog box, look for the *Name* zone at the bottom, and type "ProductsManagementMVVMViewModel". Click the *Add* button.
- Replace the ProductsManagementMVVMViewModel class code with the following one:

```
public class ProductsManagementMVVMViewModel
  : Notifier
{
  #region Input and output properties

  private string searchInput;

  public string SearchInput
  {
    get { return searchInput; }
    set
    {
```

```csharp
      searchInput = value;
      base.OnPropertyChanged("SearchInput");
      OnSearchInputChanged();
    }
  }

  private IEnumerable<Product> foundProducts;

  public IEnumerable<Product> FoundProducts
  {
    get { return foundProducts; }
    set
    {
      foundProducts = value;
      OnPropertyChanged("FoundProducts");
    }
  }

  private Product selectedProduct;

  public Product SelectedProduct
  {
    get { return selectedProduct; }
    set
    {
      selectedProduct = value;
      OnPropertyChanged("SelectedProduct");
    }
  }

  #endregion
```

```csharp
ProductsFactory factory = new ProductsFactory();

public ProductsManagementMVVMViewModel()
{
  // Optional: we're just making sure the
  // list is empty.
  FoundProducts = Enumerable.Empty<Product>();
}

private void OnSearchInputChanged()
{
  // Optional: just make sure any selected
  // product is unselected
  SelectedProduct = null;

  FoundProducts = factory.FindProducts(SearchInput);
}
}
```

- Build the solution.
- Open the *ProductsManagementMVVM.xaml* file.
- Add the following attribute to the Page element:

```
xmlns:vm="clr-namespace:BikeShop"
```

- Add the following *DataContext* property under the Page element:

## MVVM pattern for WPF

```
<Page ...>
  <Page.DataContext>
    <vm:ProductsManagementMVVMViewModel />
  </Page.DataContext>
  ...
</Page>
```

- Add the following attribute to the TextBox control:

```
Text="{Binding SearchInput, Mode=TwoWay,
UpdateSourceTrigger=PropertyChanged}"
```

> *UpdateSourceTrigger* is here so that the *SearchInput* property is updated immediately whenever a character is typed into the TextBox control. Otherwise, the *SearchInput* property would be updated only when focus is lost.

- Add the following attributes to the DataGrid control:

```
ItemsSource="{Binding FoundProducts}"
SelectedItem="{Binding SelectedProduct, Mode=TwoWay}"
```

- Add the following attribute to the Border control:

```
DataContext="{Binding SelectedProduct}"
```

- Add the following code inside the *Border* element:

```
<StackPanel Margin="10">
  <TextBlock Text="Product details"
    FontWeight="Bold"
    FontSize="16"
    HorizontalAlignment="Center"
    Margin="10" />
  <TextBlock Text="Title" />
  <TextBox Text="{Binding Title, Mode=TwoWay}" />
  <TextBlock Text="Price" />
  <TextBox Text="{Binding Price, Mode=TwoWay}" />
  <TextBlock Text="Color" />
  <TextBox Text="{Binding Color, Mode=TwoWay}" />
  <Border Background="{Binding Color}"
    Height="10" />
  <TextBlock Text="Reference" />
  <TextBox Text="{Binding Reference, Mode=TwoWay}" />
</StackPanel>
```

- Open the *Menu.xaml.cs* file.
- Locate the following code:

```
NavigationService.Navigate(
  new Uri("/ProductsManagement.xaml",
    UriKind.Relative)
);
```

- Replace it with the following code:

```
NavigationService.Navigate(
  new Uri("/ProductsManagementMVVM.xaml",
    UriKind.Relative)
);
```

- Run the application (click on the *Debug / Start Debugging* menu entry).
- Click on the "Products" button. Type a search string. Check that when you select an product from the *DataGrid* control all of its properties are displayed on the right-hand side panel.
- Change some product properties using the right-hand side panel. Check that the changes are displayed in the *DataGrid* control.
- Close the application.

## 6.11 MVVM frameworks in short

Using the MVVM pattern requires some plumbing work, like coding notifying properties, implementing *INotifyPropertyChanged*, writing the XAML that triggers method calls, instantiating the ViewModel and assigning it to the View. Plus you may need dependency injection including for the ViewModel or a way to communicate between the views.

MVVM frameworks are here for one main purpose: make the above tasks easier and less verbose. There are several MVVM frameworks, and any of them brings you:

- a *ViewModelBase*[4] class from which you inherit in order to create a ViewModel, that implements *INotifyPropertyChanged*;
- property change notification that limits errors (stating the property name as a string is error-prone) and ensure that the notification is not raised on a worker thread;
- a *DelegateCommand*[5] class which you can use in order to easily create commands, should you decide to use commands.

Plus, MVVM frameworks can offer some more niceties like Visual Studio snippets for notifying properties and templates for views and ViewModels.

Among the frameworks worth of attention are the following:

- Prism: made by the Microsoft Patterns and Practices team, it also offers a very detailed guide about modular application architecture and many bricks

---
[4] Exact name varies according to the framework.
[5] Exact name varies according to the framework.

that can prove useful for logging, routing or dependency injection.
- MVVM Light: offers Visual Studio templates.
- Caliburn.Micro: available for almost all XAML platforms (WPF, UWP, Silverlight), simplifies your code if you follow its conventions.

Try them and decide of your own favorite. I've used those three frameworks over several projects and *Caliburn.Micro* has become my favorite because it simplifies XAML a lot when you follow its conventions. For instance, if a method has the same name as a control it is automatically invoked when the control raises its main event, and you can manipulate ViewModels while views are automatically instantiated and assigned their ViewModel. But it all boils down to a matter of taste and I'm sure you'll find your own favorite.

# A word from the author

I sincerely hope you enjoyed reading this book as much as I liked writing it and that you quickly become proficient enough with WPF and the MVVM pattern.

If you would like to get in touch you can use :

- email: books@aweil.fr
- Facebook: https://facebook.com/learncollection

In case your project needs it, I'm also available for speaking, teaching, consulting and coding, all around the world.

If you liked this book, you probably saved a lot of time thanks to it. I'd be very grateful if you took some minutes of your precious time to leave a comment on the site where you purchased this book. Thanks a ton!

# The Learn collection

This book is part of the *Learn collection*.

The *Learn collection* allows developers to self-teach new technologies in a matter of days.

**Published books**

- Learn ASP.NET Core MVC[6]
- Learn ASP.NET MVC[7]
- Learn Meteor[8]
- Learn WPF MVVM[9]

**To be published**

- Learn Xamarin
- Learn Universal Windows

---

[6] https://leanpub.com/netcore
[7] https://leanpub.com/aspnetmvc
[8] https://leanpub.com/learnmeteor
[9] https://leanpub.com/learnwpf

Printed in Great Britain
by Amazon